Dear
Margaret,
Today
I
Died . . .

Dear Margaret, Today I Died . . .

Letters from Vietnam
by LTC Oscar Herrgesell
Compiled by Margaret Rowton Herrgesell

The Naylor Company
Book Publishers of the Southwest
San Antonio, Texas

Library of Congress Cataloging in Publication Data

Herrgesell, Oscar, 1926-1972
Dear Margaret, today I died . . .

1 Vietnamese Conflict, 1961- —Personal narratives, American.
2. Herrgesell, Oscar, 1926-1972. 3. Herrgesell, Margaret Rowton.
I. Herrgesell, Margaret Rowton. II. Title.
DS557.A69H37 959.704'38 73-23044
ISBN 0-8111-0526-1

Printed in the United States of America

Dedication

To the memory of those U.S. servicemen who came back in a box, and certainly to their families, I dedicate this book.

Where have all the flowers gone?
When will they learn?
When will they ever learn.

List of Illustrations

LTC and Mrs. Oscar Herrgesell

MAJ Oscar Herrgesell receives the Bronze Star Medal

Promotion received January 15, 1968

Evaluation duty at Camp Ripley, Minn., 1971

Posthumous awards presented to Mrs. Herrgesell

By direction of the President

THE AIR MEDAL
(Posthumously)

is presented to

LIEUTENANT COLONEL OSCAR HERRGESELL
United States Army

Lieutenant Colonel Oscar Herrgesell distinguished himself by meritorious achievement during sustained aerial operational activities against hostile forces in the Republic of Vietnam during the period 3 May 1972 to 9 July 1972. The courage, outstanding achievements, and dynamic leadership demonstrated by Colonel Herrgesell while participating in aerial flight under extremely hazardous conditions were of the highest order. During this period Colonel Herrgesell participated as a noncrew member of an Army aircraft in more than twenty-five combat operational or aerial reconnaissance missions in the combat zone or over hostile territory. At all times he displayed the highest order of air discipline and acted in accordance with the highest traditions of the United States Army. The outstanding degree of professionalism and selfless devotion to duty displayed by Lieutenant Colonel Herrgesell reflected credit upon himself and the military service.

Citation for receiving the Air Medal

THE UNITED STATES OF AMERICA

TO ALL WHO SHALL SEE THESE PRESENTS, GREETING:
THIS IS TO CERTIFY THAT
THE PRESIDENT OF THE UNITED STATES OF AMERICA
AUTHORIZED BY EXECUTIVE ORDER, MAY 11, 1942
HAS AWARDED

THE AIR MEDAL

TO

LIEUTENANT COLONEL OSCAR HERRGESELL, UNITED STATES ARMY

FOR MERITORIOUS ACHIEVEMENT
WHILE PARTICIPATING IN AERIAL FLIGHT
IN VIETNAM FROM 3 MAY 1972 TO 9 JULY 1972

GIVEN UNDER MY HAND IN THE CITY OF WASHINGTON
THIS 21ST DAY OF DECEMBER 19 72

VERNE L. BOWERS
Major General, USA
The Adjutant General

SECRETARY OF THE ARMY

Certificate for receiving the Air Medal

CITATION

BY DIRECTION OF THE PRESIDENT

THE BRONZE STAR MEDAL
(FIRST OAK LEAF CLUSTER)

IS PRESENTED POSTHUMOUSLY TO

LIEUTENANT COLONEL OSCAR HERRGESELL, UNITED STATES ARMY

FOR DISTINGUISHING HIMSELF BY OUTSTANDING MERITORIOUS SERVICE IN CONNECTION WITH GROUND OPERATIONS AGAINST A HOSTILE FORCE IN THE REPUBLIC OF VIETNAM DURING THE PERIOD

7 MAY 1972 TO 23 JUNE 1972

THROUGH HIS UNTIRING EFFORTS AND PROFESSIONAL ABILITY, HE CONSISTENTLY OBTAINED OUTSTANDING RESULTS. HE WAS QUICK TO GRASP THE IMPLICATION OF NEW PROBLEMS WITH WHICH HE WAS FACED AS A RESULT OF THE EVER CHANGING SITUATIONS INHERENT IN A COUNTERINSURGENCY OPERATION AND TO FIND WAYS AND MEANS TO SOLVE THOSE PROBLEMS. THE ENERGETIC APPLICATION OF HIS EXTENSIVE KNOWLEDGE HAS MATERIALLY CONTRIBUTED TO THE EFFORTS OF THE UNITED STATES MISSION TO THE REPUBLIC OF VIETNAM TO ASSIST THAT COUNTRY IN RIDDING ITSELF OF THE COMMUNIST THREAT TO ITS FREEDOM. HIS INITIATIVE, ZEAL, SOUND JUDGMENT AND DEVOTION TO DUTY HAVE BEEN IN THE HIGHEST TRADITION OF THE UNITED STATES ARMY AND REFLECT GREAT CREDIT ON HIMSELF, HIS UNIT AND THE MILITARY SERVICE.

Citation for receiving the Bronze Star Medal
(First Oak Leaf Cluster)

THE UNITED STATES OF AMERICA

TO ALL WHO SHALL SEE THESE PRESENTS, GREETING:

THIS IS TO CERTIFY THAT
THE PRESIDENT OF THE UNITED STATES OF AMERICA
AUTHORIZED BY EXECUTIVE ORDER, 24 AUGUST 1962
HAS AWARDED

THE BRONZE STAR MEDAL

(FIRST OAK LEAF CLUSTER)
TO

LIEUTENANT COLONEL OSCAR HERRGESELL, UNITED STATES ARMY

FOR
MERITORIOUS ACHIEVEMENT
IN GROUND OPERATIONS AGAINST HOSTILE FORCES
IN VIETNAM FROM 7 MAY 1972 TO 23 JUNE 1972
GIVEN UNDER MY HAND IN THE CITY OF WASHINGTON
THIS 7TH DAY OF FEBRUARY 19 73

VERNE L. BOWERS
Major General, USA
The Adjutant General

UNITED STATES OF AMERICA
WAR OFFICE

SECRETARY OF THE ARMY

Certificate for receiving the Bronze Star Medal
(First Oak Leaf Cluster)

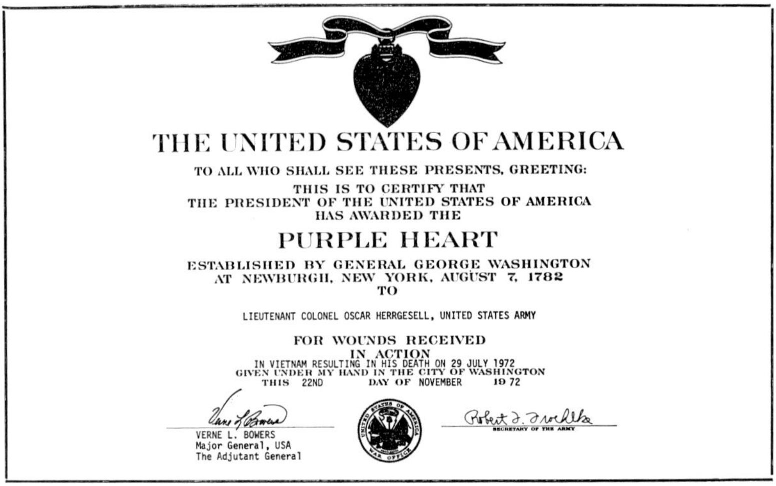

THE UNITED STATES OF AMERICA

TO ALL WHO SHALL SEE THESE PRESENTS, GREETING:

THIS IS TO CERTIFY THAT
THE PRESIDENT OF THE UNITED STATES OF AMERICA
HAS AWARDED THE

PURPLE HEART

ESTABLISHED BY GENERAL GEORGE WASHINGTON
AT NEWBURGH, NEW YORK, AUGUST 7, 1782
TO

LIEUTENANT COLONEL OSCAR HERRGESELL, UNITED STATES ARMY

FOR WOUNDS RECEIVED
IN ACTION
IN VIETNAM RESULTING IN HIS DEATH ON 29 JULY 1972
GIVEN UNDER MY HAND IN THE CITY OF WASHINGTON
THIS 22ND DAY OF NOVEMBER 19 72

VERNE L. BOWERS
Major General, USA
The Adjutant General

SECRETARY OF THE ARMY

Certificate for receiving the Purple Heart

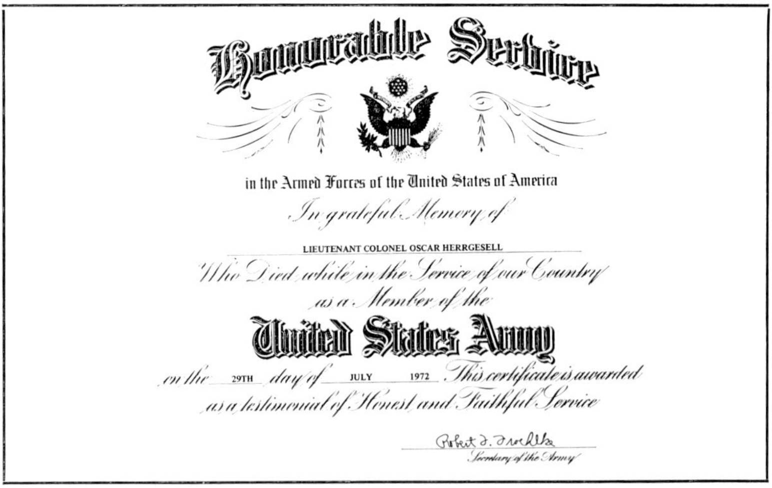

Honorable Service

in the Armed Forces of the United States of America

In grateful Memory of

LIEUTENANT COLONEL OSCAR HERRGESELL

Who Died while in the Service of our Country
as a Member of the

United States Army

on the 29TH day of JULY 1972 This certificate is awarded
as a testimonial of Honest and Faithful Service

Secretary of the Army

Certificate of Honorable Service

The President of the United States of America, authorized by Executive Order, 16 January 1969, has awarded the Meritorious Service Medal to

LIEUTENANT COLONEL OSCAR HERRGESELL, UNITED STATES ARMY

for outstanding meritorious service:

Lieutenant Colonel Herrgesell, Infantry, distinguished himself by outstanding meritorious service while assigned to the US Army Advisor Group (ARNGUS), Indiana, from November 1969 to November 1971. Serving as Army Advisor, 76th Brigade, 38th Infantry Division, Indiana Army National Guard, he displayed unusual initiative, professional competence, and sound judgment in the performance of his complex duties and achieved optimum results. Through his detailed knowledge of training principles and techniques, and his exceptional ability to impart clear, concise instructions, he enabled the units he served to achieve outstanding progress in organization, administration and training. By his unfailing devotion to duty and practiced diplomacy in association with personnel of the Indiana Army National Guard, he contributed immeasurably to the smooth accomplishment of the mission of the US Army Advisor Group (ARNGUS). Colonel Herrgesell's enthusiastic application of military and professional knowledge, pride in accomplishment, and ability to produce results of the highest caliber reflect great credit upon himself and the military service.

Citation for receiving the Meritorious Service Medal

western union **Telegram**

JZA038(1053)(1-0075440215)PD 08/02/72 1049
ICS IPMJZEB JKS
ZCZC 078 A EF CT ACB05 XV INTER FR USGOVT PDB DTL TDCT AC WASHINGTON D
RMS 08-02 1036A EDT
MRS LULA M HERRGESELL, DLY 1.50 DONT PHONE IF MOVED DLR AND WIRE
COLL NEW ADS 220 EDGEWOOD TERRACE / JACKSON MISSISSIPPI

THE SECRETARY OF THE ARMY HAS ASKED ME TO EXPRESS HIS DEEP REGRET THAT YOU HUSBAND, LIEUTENANT COLONEL OSCAR HERRGESELL, WAS KILLED IN ACTION IN VIETNAM ON 29 JULY 1972. HE WAS A PASSENGER ON A MILITARY AIRCRAFT ON A MILITARY MISSION WHEN THE AIRCRAFT RECEIVED GROUND FIRE FROM A HOSTILE FORCE. THE AIRCRAFT CRASHED BUT DID NOT BURN. HE WAS PREVIOUSLY REPORTED AS MISSING IN ACTION. HIS REMAINS HAVE BEEN RECOVERED AND POSITIVELY IDENTIFIED. PLEASE ACCEPT MY DEEPEST SYMPATHY. THIS CONFIRMS PERSONAL NOTIFICATION MADE BY A REPRESENTATIVE OF THE SECRETARY OF THE ARMY

Telegram of sympathy from Verne L. Bowers, the Adjutant General

7 August 1972

Colonel HOÀNG-ĐỨC-NINH
Commanding Officer
44th Special Tactical Zone
APO 3893
Republic of Vietnam

To :

Mrs MARGARET HERRGESELL
220 Edgewood Terrace
APT P 21
Jackson, Mississipi 39.206
U S A

Dear Mrs Herrgesell

It is with deep regret that I have to write this letter. Your husband's death on 29th of July will be a loss for you, the United States, and us, the people of Vietnam. We are deeply saddened by his loss.

LTC Herrgesell was well known and very respected by all who served with him, especially among the Vietnamese soldiers. We have lost a brave friend who unselfishly aided the Vietnamese people.

As the Commanding Officer of 44th STZ, I would like to express my deep and sincere sympathy for your loss.

Sincerely,

BIỆT-KHU 44

Letter of sympathy from
COL Hoàng-Dúc-Ninh

8 August 1972

Dear Mrs. Herrgesell:

It was with sadness that I learned of the passing of your husband, Lieutenant Colonel Oscar Herrgesell, on 29 July, in Vietnam.

Although you must be suffering the most heartbreaking sorrow, may the kind thoughts and prayers of all your "Army family" bring you some comfort during the trying days ahead. The memory of your husband and his devoted service to the Army and the Nation will be long remembered by his comrades in arms as we continue to carry on the task in which he shared our highest aims and goals -- defending the right of men to choose their own destiny and to live in dignity and freedom.

All members of the Army join in expressing sympathy to you and your son.

Sincerely,

BRUCE PALMER, JR.
General, U. S. Army
Acting Chief of Staff

Letter of sympathy from
GEN Bruce Palmer

DEPARTMENT OF THE ARMY
OFFICE OF THE CHAPLAIN
Headquarters U.S. Army Support Element MR IV
APO San Francisco 96215

AVBAWV-CH

8 August 1972

Mrs. Oscar Herrgesell
220 Edgewood Terrace
P-21
Jackson, Mississippi 39206

Dear Mrs. Herrgesell:

I wish to extend to you my sincere sympathy during your time of sorrow over the death of your husband. Words can do very little to help ease the hurt caused by saddness and loneliness when a loved one dies. I do hope that it will be of some comfort to you to know that all the men here who knew and worked with your husband highly respected his dedication and devotion to duty. We all share in your sorrow.

I conducted the Memorial Service for your husband, LTC Herrgesell. It was a very simple but dignified service held outside during the late afternoon hours. The service was attended by members of Advisory Teams 50 and 84, by the Deputy Commanding General of DRAC and by Vietnamese friends. I am enclosing the Memorial Service bulletin.

Be assured that our prayers will be with you during the painful days and weeks ahead. My prayer is that even in the face of death, God will grant you strength and courage to face the future without your husband and in so doing find a new life for yourself.

Sincerely,

DAVID O. GOLDEN
Chaplain (CPT), USA
Deputy Staff Chaplain, ASE IV

Letter of sympathy from
David O. Golden, Chaplain

REPUBLIC OF VIETNAM
MINISTRY OF DEFENSE
JOINT GENERAL STAFF/RVNAF
RANGER COMMAND

10 Aug 72

Mrs Margaret Hergessell
220 Edgewood Terrace, Apt T-21
Jackson, Mississippi 39206

Dear Mrs Hergessell,

The officers and men of the Ranger Command, Republic of Vietnam Armed Forces, join with me in extending to you our deepest sympathy on the death of your husband, Lieutenant Colonel Oscar Hergessell.

I realize that words can do little to relieve the suffering of you and your family in this time of sorrow. After nearly two decades of bloodshed and the loss of tens of thousands of brave American and Vietnamese fighting men, it is even more difficult to understand and accept the loss of such courageous people as your husband. While the combat role of most Americans has been eliminated, others as advisors continue to fight side by side with our forces. Their efforts, their advise, and their actions often go unheralded although the hazards they share with us are as real as at any time during this war.

We Vietnamese owe an immeasurable debt of gratitude to all American soldiers who have fought in our cause, but those who have served as advisors will always have a special place of honor in our hearts. In a way which is difficult to understand, and even more difficult to describe, the spirit of the American advisor is the cornerstone upon which we have depended in our fight to build a lasting peace. The advisor lives and works with our fighting men twenty four hours a day. A few, like your husband, Lieutenant Colonel Oscar Hergessell, make the supreme sacrifice and die, shoulder to shoulder, with them.

I want to assure you that your husband's loss is mourned on both sides of the ocean. We respected him as a man. We salute him as a soldier.

Sincerely yours,

NGUYEN QUANG KIET
COL, INF
Commanding

Letter of sympathy from
COL Nguyen Quang Kiet

THE WHITE HOUSE

WASHINGTON

August 17, 1972

Dear Mrs. Herrgesell:

Mrs. Nixon joins me in expressing our deepest sympathy on the tragic loss of your husband, Lieutenant Colonel Oscar Herrgesell.

No words can bring you solace, but the end of this cruel war will forever remain a tribute to your husband's immeasurable sacrifice in the cause of freedom for his fellow men. All Americans honor his memory, and I hope that his great courage and his brave response to our country's call will strengthen and comfort you in the days ahead.

Sincerely,

Richard Nixon

Mrs. Oscar Herrgesell
220 Edgewood Terrace
Apartment 21
Jackson, Mississippi 39206

Letter of sympathy from
President Nixon

HEA ERS
UNITED STATES MILITAR CE COMMAND, VIETNAM
OFFICE C MANDER
APO SAN O 96222

27 AUG 1972

Mrs. Oscar Herrgesell
220 Edgewood Terrace, Apartment 21
Jackson, Mississippi 39202

Dear Mrs. Herrgesell:

On behalf of the U.S. Military Assistance Command, Vietnam, I wish to extend my sympathy to you over the loss of your husband, Lieutenant Colonel Oscar Herrgesell, United States Army, and express my condolences during your time of sorrow and bereavement.

It is my hope that you will find a measure of solace in knowing your husband lost his life serving his country. May your faith sustain you in these difficult moments and provide the strength and courage to help you overcome the tragic loss you have suffered.

Sincerely,

Fred C. Weyand

FRED C. WEYAND
General, USA
Commanding

Letter of sympathy from
GEN Fred C. Weyand

SECRETARY OF THE ARMY
WASHINGTON

September 8, 1972

Dear Mrs. Herrgesell:

Please accept my deepest sympathy for the death of your husband, Lieutenant Colonel Oscar Herrgesell, in Vietnam on July 29, 1972.

We are proud of his military accomplishments and grateful to him for his contribution to our Nation's strength. All members of the United States Army join me in expressing the hope that the memory of his dedicated service will help to ease your sorrow.

Sincerely yours,

Robert F. Froehlke

Robert F. Froehlke

Mrs. Oscar Herrgesell
220 Edgewood Terrace
Apartment 21
Jackson, Mississippi 39206

Letter of sympathy from Robert F. Froehlke, Secretary of the Army

DEPARTMENT OF THE ARMY
OFFICE OF THE ADJUTANT GENERAL
WASHINGTON, D.C. 20314

DAAG-PSA-BC

13 February 1973

Mrs. Lula Herrgesell
220 Edgewood Terrace, Apt. 21
Jackson, Mississippi 39206

Dear Mrs. Herrgesell:

I have the honor to inform you that your husband has been awarded posthumously the Bronze Star Medal (First Oak Leaf Cluster), Air Medal and the Purple Heart.

Prior to his death he had been awarded the Bronze Star Medal, Meritorious Service Medal, United Nations Service Medal, Korean Service Medal, National Defense Service Medal, Vietnam Service Medal, Vietnam Campaign Medal, Combat Infantryman Badge and the Parachutist Badge.

A representative of the Commander, Third United States Army will contact you to make arrangements for the presentation ceremony in accordance with your wishes.

My sympathy is with you in your great loss.

Sincerely,

for Edward L. Cary, Major

PETER O'BRIEN
Colonel, AGC
Chief, Personnel Actions
Division, TAGO

Letter advising of posthumous awards

LTC Oscar Herrgesell

19 February 1972

Hi Sweetheart,

Arrived here at Long Binh this morning, and thought I had better write a few lines while I have the time.

We left Travis AFB, yesterday, February 17, at 7 P.M. in the evening. After crossing the International Date Line, the time changes, and we arrived here around 8:30 today, the nineteenth. Had a good flight, but so long!

We had brief stops at Hawaii and Okinawa, so I had time to make a few calls to some friends. The weather in Hawaii was really nice; about sixty-nine degrees at ten o'clock in the evening.

This morning we had the routine briefing, and processed in. I was issued five sets of jungle fatigues, and all the accessories. I should have just brought along my shaving kit! Haven't been off post, as we are restricted, partly (I think) to keep people from going out and around "lobbying" for a job. I don't know what I will get, but expectations aren't very high. I think I will just wait and see before I start to complain, as I just might make out okay.

As expected, everything is in somewhat of a turmoil here. At least it doesn't appear to be as well organized as it was before, what with the shortage of personnel.

So far, the food is good, and the PX has a fairly good

supply of essentials, at least here at Long Binh. Had to cash in all our U.S. money, and get "Funny Money" instead.

Right now, I am sitting in the Transient Quarters on my cot, sweating, and waiting for mealtime, and for new patches to be sewn on my uniforms. Should be all set then, and will probably have orders tomorrow or the next day.

Out of approximately two hundred people, I was the only LTC, one MAJ, and the rest CPT's, LT's, and EM. Many of them have been here before, too, but to some it is exciting, and visions of jeep escorts with machine guns.

I am processing in at the same place I processed out of, in 1967. It hasn't changed much, and brings back a lot of memories. Right here, we are close to an airstrip, so we constantly hear helicopters, other planes, and vehicles. I must get used to all that noise again, but it will only take a few days to become acclimated to all the hubbub.

I hope you can read this, as I am writing on my knee, plus the fact that I am very tired.

Enough about me! Hope this finds you okay, moved into the apartment, and busy as a beaver. I will write more about what is going on, when I get to where I am going. Miss you and am thinking of you always. Until next time, all my love to you.

Oscar

23 February 1972

Hi Sweetheart,

I'm at Long Binh, which is about ten miles north of Saigon, and I guess that I will be here for awhile. You wouldn't believe this place! It covers about eight to ten miles with barracks, airfields, and supply depots. Where I am, there are a lot of two-story barracks, somewhat like the WW II barracks, but with individual rooms, all about 10x12 feet in size, and plenty of hot shower water!! I will be in this building temporarily, until a trailer becomes vacant, and then I will have one half of a trailer. How about that? I don't know what they look like inside, but at least there will be some privacy. Being on this post is just like being stateside, as they have just about anything you can think of, although the work schedule (seven days a week, 7:30 to 7:00) will not allow much time for anything else. They have lighted tennis courts, swimming pool, large PX, a large post office, and a Chase Manhattan Bank, operated by Vietnamese. They have let things get rundown, though, from all appearances.

The place I'm assigned to will be one of the last out if I stick with them. I guess there aren't too many jobs for an Infantry LTC right now. At present, I have a job as a special assistant to a Supply COL, at the Army Depot here. We are going to be doing a lot of shipping out within the next six months, so I guess I'll be somewhat of a co-ordinator, pushing, kicking, and taking names. Doesn't sound too interesting, but there is plenty of work to do, so at least I can be accomplishing something worthwhile if I can be of any help in getting most of the stuff moved out. You wouldn't believe the amount of junk piled up here! When I say junk, I don't mean to imply that it isn't good. Some is old, but there is an awful lot of new stuff also, many miles of it, and a great number of huge warehouses stacked full. Something like 200,000 *tons*! So you can see that we will have much to do. It isn't the sort of job I would have picked at all, and probably not too good career-wise, but maybe we can clean this up in four to five months, and then something better will be available.

Today, Sammy Davis, Jr. is putting on a show or two. Some of the men went to see it, and said it was real great.

Right now, I'm still processing in. Most of the wheels are busy and it's hard to get in to see them about details of assignments, so you can see that it all takes time. Tomorrow I hope to get to Finance to get everything in that department squared away. I should be able to get by on $150 per month, and that includes buying a gift now and then. Eating in the Field Mess costs about $1.50 per day; maid service, which includes laundry, polishing shoes, and cleaning room, runs $10 per month. Not bad, huh?

So far, I have run into only one old acquaintance. The chief of staff of Saigon Support Command, of which I am a member, was in the same class with me at Fort Leavenworth. He is now a COL and has a pretty good job.

The Americans who spent their tours here before hardly knew there was a war going on. Quite a bit different from being out in the field, although I think I would rather be out, but the Americans are not too involved in that anymore, and it's probably a good thing.

I haven't gotten around here much yet, so there isn't much else I can tell you. I have a PACEX catalog that I will mail in a few days. Look through it, and start a list of things that you would like to have. We will get our order in early, in case things go too fast.

Am wondering what you are doing, how you are, and, of course, missing you a whole bunch. Otherwise, I'm in great shape.

Until next time, all my love to you.

Oscar

25 February 1972

Hi Sweetheart,

Well, here it is Friday, though I must admit that over here that doesn't make any difference. I moved today to my final (for awhile, anyway) stop. You wouldn't believe it! Have a nice two-bedroom trailer, which I am sharing with a COL (Dr.) who seems to be a real nice person. It has a nice asphalt tile floor, excellent bathroom with tub/shower combination, two air-conditioners, electric lights, electric refrigerator, matching gas stove, plenty of pantry space, and a double sink. The living room/kitchen has a couch, chair, dinette table with four chairs, a desk, bookshelves, end tables, lamps, and the COL has a small TV set. Our rooms are separated by the bath. Inside the trailer, we have two large plants. One is about two feet high and loaded with red peppers; the other one is about four feet high, with little tiny oranges about the size of a golf ball, and some are ripe! Now, how about all that? I am within walking distance of the Field Ration Mess and the Officers' Club. Also have my own jeep to use now, so you can see that I'm in good shape. Something is bound to happen, as this is too good to last. I do think this place will be cleared out in June or July.

Right now, I'm involved in trying to get approximately

20,000 CONEX containers shipped out, repaired or junked. In case you don't know what they are, they are metal containers used to ship things in; most are about twice the size of the Dempsey Dumpster containers used in the States. Hope I can get rid of them, but it will take some time, I'm sure.

There are a lot of American civilians working over here at Long Binh. They are contractors, and a lot of GS types. I imagine that many of them will be leaving soon.

The more I see of the Supply Depot, the more amazed I am at all the equipment and junk that the U.S. has hauled over here, used and abused! It is really unbelievable. There is all kind of equipment in all manner of condition – new, used, broken, unidentified, and lost. It is not too difficult to see where the old American dollar goes in a war like this.

As soon as I get time, and into some sort of a schedule, I will get squared away and start some correspondence.

I failed to pick up my pay record at Finance, so I'll have to write to Stout Field and ask them to request Fort Benjamin Harrison to send it on. When I was there, they gave me the impression that it should stay there, but now I find that that was a mistake.

They tell me that it is easy to get in a MARS telephone call from here, so I'll be trying to call you before long. For me to get in a call to you at 4:00 P.M. in Jackson, I would have to "book" the call at 0600 here in the morning. We are about ten hours behind you, so I will probably be calling you in the evening, if all works according to schedule.

I think about you all the time, and miss you most of all in the evening, when the day is over. Take care of yourself, and remember that someone over here loves you very much. SHAPE UP!

Oscar

2 March 1972

Hi Darling,

It was good to hear your voice on the telephone yesterday, even though I forgot many of the things I wanted to say. Next time, I will have some notes handy!

Have had a busy day today. The workers didn't show up on time, nor did they want to work much, the right equipment wasn't available, and it seemed like nothing went right. Maybe tomorrow will be better.

Right now, I should be out eating, but the COL went off to some class tonight, and I can't find the key to lock the trailer. Guess I'll have to wait until he returns, because I can't go off and leave it unlocked, as someone might come in and steal everything. I haven't had time to stock up the grocery pantry, yet.

I'm glad to hear that you are working occasionally. That will help to make the time go by quickly.

Yesterday, I found the time to visit the Post Library. It is about four times the size of the one at Killeen Base. There were GI's working there in the evening, when I was there. Surprisingly, they had about one hundred periodicals, and about fifty leading newspapers! So, I sat down and read the *Indianapolis Star*. How about that? Occasionally, they have a number "85" movie, usually old and garbled.

There are some pretty nice people at the Depot where I am working, but they do not have a "unit spirit" that I can see. Haven't met too many people off duty, as a result of the long working hours, but no sweat. I have things to read, PT, and letters to write.

These Viets are something else! They are very slow, not worried, and no sense of urgency. Can't get most of them to hurry, unless you really talk tough to them right off, and then they stay somewhat straight. If one doesn't talk tough, they think you are easy, and don't respect you at all. It seems like that Uncle Sam has hired a million of them, and maybe ten of them will do a little work. But most of this is the GI's fault. They have kids trying to supervise them; kids who are hardly capable of taking care of themselves, so the Viets take advantage of the situation.

I hope you have received the PACEX catalog, and have a list started.

Hey – I miss you! Takes a lot of time to get used to being apart. But I keep busy, and think about when we will be together again.

Say hello to the kids, and everyone else for me.

Until next time, all my love to you.

Oscar

Sunday 4:00 P.M.

Hi Sweetheart,

Hope this finds you in good shape and settled down somewhat. I'm starting to get my feet on the ground a little, but it will take some time. I just found out that I have to make a bunker line inspection tonight, from midnight until three in the morning, so I guess that will just about take care of tonight.

Attended church this morning out here where I work. The chaplain, a nice young major, holds services out here in the conference room. There was just a few of us there, so it was very informal. He had a little tape recorder, on which he had recorded the hymn for the day, and he played it, while we sang along with it. That way, no one was embarrassed by singing off-key!

Finally had a few minutes to go by the PX concession buildings today. They don't have any of the large teakwood elephants we were interested in, but they do have some of the large ceramic ones, about two feet high, with the flat top. I'm thinking of sending a couple of them home, to use in the den or on a patio.

If things stay the way they are, I can take a fourteen-day leave, after six months, or a seven-day R & R plus seven-day leave, either in Hawaii, Taiwan, or Bangkok. It is early yet, but we can start thinking about it, as requests must go in a couple of months in advance. Also, if the tour here gets cut short, we might miss out, and we don't want that to happen, right?

I checked on buying film for my Minolta camera, and they don't carry it over here, so guess I'll have to ask you to send me some. If I ever get to the main PX in Saigon, I might be able to find some. This PX is pretty good, but not many brands to select from. For example, they have shelves of Colgate toothpaste and Lux soap, but no other choice. I guess we are lucky to get that.

Guess what? They even have a place one can call, and have hot food delivered to your hootch by a Vietnamese on a Honda! I imagine the concession is located here on post, but I haven't checked it out.

My roommate has planted some tomato plants in a cardboard box. How about that?

Another thing they have over here, which I have never seen before, is a "throw away" barbecue grill. It has folded-up wire legs, wire mesh on top, and charcoal packed inside, ready to light. It is large enough for a couple of good-sized steaks. O.K., huh?

Am running out of time, so will stop for now. Until next time, all my love to you.

Your Oscar

Thursday 9 March 9:00 P.M.

Hi Sweetheart,

Received your nice letter today. (The one with Charles' letter in it.) I know you are glad to be settled down somewhat, and I am sorry you had so much trouble. I am also sorry that we could not be together on our second anniversary, but I'm glad we are both well, and can hopefully look forward to many together in the future, right?

I stopped at the PX today, and bought two rib-eye steaks, some tomatoes, and cucumbers. Saturday, if I have time, I'll cook a good steak dinner. Sounds good, huh?

Right now, everything is dirty here. When I come in at night, my clothes and hair are filled with dirt, so a good shower really feels great!

My day begins around 6:30 A.M., and I return from work around 6:00 P.M., do PT for about an hour, shower, read, go to dinner, return to the trailer, write a letter or read some more before going to sleep. So far, I'm halfway through the New Testament.

Do you realize that I've been gone almost a month already? First thing you know, we will be back together again!

Our maid has only been working for about two months, and doesn't speak English, but she does a good job on the clothes, and generally in the hootch, so no complaints.

I've been thinking about buying all the kids a ring while over here. What do you think about that for their Christmas gifts?

Before long, it will be warm enough for you to go swimming in Mississippi, right? I haven't had time to get over to the pool here, yet.

Not much news from here today. Oh, I was happy to hear your lovely voice when we talked on the seventh! It made me feel good the whole day!

Remember I'll always love you, and am so happy that we found each other. All my love to you.

Your Oscar

Sunday 12 March 5.00 P.M.

Hi Darling,

Since I have access to an electric typewriter, will take advantage of it and get a short note off to you. At least we have some decent office furniture here.

Have had a busy day, just doing the usual routine things. Went to church this morning, in the conference room. As soon as I get this job where things are running smoothly, I will start going over to one of the chapels on the main part of post. I'm getting the job organized pretty well now, where I don't have to be there every minute watching things.

I stopped over at the PX concessions at noon today. Think I'll send two of the large brass candle holders, a couple of the large elephants, and a brass table. I don't want to wait too long, because some of the concessions are having their contracts terminated, and some items will no longer be available. I looked at a beautiful teakwood coffee table. It is hand carved, with a glass top, and four stools, shaped like a piece of pie, that fit under the table when not in use. I don't know where we would put it, but it is going to be hard to pass up. Also dropped by the tailor shop, and looked around, as they advertise a tailor-made double knit suit for fifty-five dollars. I asked the tailor where the material was from, and he said the States. Think I'll check that one out.

My records from Finance, Fort Benjamin Harrison, have not arrived here yet, so I haven't received travel pay, or dislocation. Don't really need it, but I could have it in savings drawing interest, right?

Am still not used to being over here. Seems like a dream, sometimes. I know where I am, and what I'm doing, but somehow, it seems unreal. Oh well, I don't care if I never get used to being over here. Not that it is so bad, but just the fact that we are apart.

I think I'll head over to the library tonight, and catch up on the news. I forgot to thank you for the Indianapolis newspaper. I am looking forward to receiving it.

I read someplace that they have a hobby shop here on post. When I get time, I want to check it out. When the troop strength gets low, many of these places will close down.

If I get a chance next week, I plan to drive in to the Tan Son Nhut Air Base, and look around.

Not much of interest to write about today, so this will be short.

By the way, how is your father making out? Hope he keeps on feeling okay.

I'm O.K., Margaret, so don't worry about me. Remember how much I love you, am thinking of you all the time, and remember you in my prayers. Keep your chin up.

Love,

Your Oscar

Thursday 16 March 8:00 P.M.

Hi Sweetie,

I dropped by the library tonight, to read for awhile, and discovered that they have some typewriters that we can use, so I will write to you. I haven't been keeping up with the news, and that is one reason that I like to come to the library and read the newspapers and magazines. It also reminds me of someone that I love very much! If I use enough imagination, I can just see you sitting behind that desk, instead of the hairy-legged G.I. in short pants and tennis shoes!

Haven't done much this week except work, and there has been enough of that, I can assure you. So far, not real hard work, but very long hours, and I am getting used to that. Actually, it's better that way, as that leaves only a couple of hours a day to call my own, so time does not drag too badly. Have been eating dinner late, so I will have to watch my weight. I miss our nice dinners together! I always looked forward to them, and really do miss them not only for the outstanding food, but for the company of someone named Margaret! Oh well, better times are to come. . . . Have to believe that, right?

On Monday, I switched on the COL's TV set, and saw the tail end of "Laugh-In." Could use a good laugh around here, now and then, so I will try to remember it next week. There isn't too much laughing around here lately. Not that things are that rough, but most people have a short-timer's attitude, and the enthusiasm for anything but getting finished and going home is "nil" in most cases. From the talk that we hear, we officers will put in the full year over here, especially since it is an election year.

Had dinner at the club last night, because I was too late at the mess hall. They serve steaks, sandwiches, and usually a $1.50 special. Anyway, I saw catfish on the menu, and decided to give them a fling. While waiting, my mind was conjuring up some real appetizing fish, but that is not what I was served! Don't know where they got it, but it came out in three big chunks, and did not even taste like catfish. It probably came off some seventy-five-pound lunker, somewhere in the Far East, but live and learn. Next time, I'll order squid or something! If I ever get to Saigon, I'm going to look for some lobster.

My "roomie" is moving to another trailer tomorrow, so unless they move another Bird Colonel in, I will get the larger room. I'm glad he is leaving. He is a nice enough guy, but he was about to drive me bananas. He puttered around in his room or the bathroom at two or three o'clock in the morning, and woke me up almost every night.

Don't know when he slept, but he sure made me lose enough. Besides that, he has junk all over the trailer. It will require a truck to move all his stuff. It is no wonder that we have five hundred people supporting one fighting man, if everyone takes that much junk around with them. Some people aren't considerate of other people at all though, and as far as I'm concerned, it is nothing more than people with super-ego, who think of none but themselves. Well, now that I have that off my chest, on with the letter!

You asked if I did any cooking? As you know, I am not the world's greatest chef, but occasionally I get my breakfast, and most of the time, I grab a snack at the trailer. Usually I have dinner at the field mess, or the officers' club. If it looks like I might stay here for several months, I might become more elaborate with my cooking, but right now, after the long days we put in, I really don't feel like spending the time off cooking some junk.

I spend most of the morning and afternoon running around in my jeep, checking, coordinating, and supervising whatever operation we may have going on at the time. After work, I get in an hour of PT, read the Bible for awhile, shower, dress, and off to the mess or club to eat. Sometime, they have a movie, but all the facilities close at ten o'clock, so everyone hits the sack. That's where I am going now. Think of you every minute, and love you most!

Oscar

Wednesday 22 March 0915 P.M.

Hello Miss Margaret,

Here I am at the library again. It is only about a half mile from where I live, so I can come over here, and type a letter, and still save time. Besides that, you can read it – right?

I hope that you are settling down somewhat. I know that I am just this week beginning to adjust to being over here. I find that if I have some little thing to look forward to during the week, it helps to make the time go by faster.

Incidentally, my "roomie" finally moved out today, so tonight I have the trailer all to myself, and have hopes of getting one good night of sleep.

I am glad that you like the plaque. I agree with you – as it was supposed to have my name and March 7 on it. Anyway, I have ordered another one, and will mail it on very soon. They are glued on, so you can remove the old one easy enough.

It has been very hot during the day, a little like the summer in Indiana.

Went down to the edge of Saigon today, to one of the ports where a lot of our junk is shipped out from. I'm just as glad to be up here where I am, because it is really dirty down there. Not like the Delta, where I was last time. They were dirty down there about a lot of things through ignorance, but they at least kept things neat and policed up, but not so up here!

You asked what is coming off out here. You probably know more about it than I do. Really, we are just trying to get things and people down to the expected level, where they can be handled properly. I am beginning to enjoy my work more, as I get to know more people, and most of them know me by now. I don't think this job will last more than a couple more months for me though. Should find out what else I might be doing, in a little while. Might get to stay right here at Long Binh.

One thing has come up at work that I will tell you about. You know how it is – people start "flapping" about something that has been in existence for years, and all of a sudden, it must be changed. Night before last I was up all night, as I had to go with other officers and NCO's to a company where they were having the problems. Was there from midnight until 5:00 A.M., slept one hour, and went to work. We have transferred the ten or twelve trouble-makers. Unbelievable, the nerve of those "punks."

The problem is they should not be handled with kid gloves, but just as everyone else. They do a weird thing called "dapping" just to irritate others, as I understand it. It is so juvenile it is disgusting.

Have a new housemate, who is really nice. He is a colonel, who came from up north, where they have closed out some of the other depots.

Found some Cornish hens at the PX, so I plan to throw one in the oven this weekend.

I am enclosing the new plate for the plaque. I hope it is satisfactory, and fits the spot.

Have been so busy this week, have not had time for PT.

Say – have you been doing any bicycle riding? I could sure use a cycle over here to get around on! I do have a jeep, and would be lost without it. A Mark III it isn't, but it gets us around.

They are flicking the lights, so I must close. Remember how I love you, and miss you so much. I pray for you, our families, and both grandchildren each night.

I am fine, so please don't worry about me. Until next time all my love to you. AND SHAPE UP!!

Your Oscar

Sunday 26 March 5:30 P.M.

Hi Sweetheart,

Here it is Sunday again, and another week down the drain. This week seemed to go pretty fast, though they can't go fast enough, right? It was a busy week, and it looks as if most of them are going to be that way. At least we have enough to do, which is more than a lot of people at USARV HQ have. They need to get rid of a bunch of them, and I think they will, starting about the first of next month.

They are having a lot of trouble in the barracks, with so-called "racial" problems. What it has amounted to so far, as near as I understand it, is that they have a percentage of blacks who have been catching some of the white soldiers asleep in their rooms or at other places, and beating them up severely, and using whatever else they can: cutting them, hitting them with clubs, etc. This has been going on for about a week, so last night they had a big fight, and now they are shaking them all down, setting patrols in the company all night. I don't know what in the world is wrong with some of the commanders in the army anymore, to allow a thing to get to that state of affairs. They are hiding behind the "racial" issue to carry on in the same manner as a gangster or hoodlum any place in the world, and should be dealt with severely, the FIRST time it happens, instead of trying to pacify it all, and end up with more trouble than you can handle. I heard a rumor that one of last week's victims had died, but you never know about that, because some people will start such rumors just to stir up more trouble. I do feel sorry for the people who are the innocent bystanders. Some of the troops have been afraid to go to sleep at night for fear of being attacked. Consequently, they are not in good shape to work the next day. When such a group of hoods rebel against authority, they should round them all up on the spot, and put them in confinement, awaiting court-martials. Instead, they pussyfoot around with those who are, in most cases, nothing more than people acting as gangsters, to the point where, when you do need to crack down on them, you look as if YOU are the agitator. I really haven't checked into it too thoroughly, but it appears to me that it can be placed on the shoulders of those commanders who have the authority, but failed to correct the situation before it got out of hand. I'm glad that I am not the troop commander, because I would not let them get away with it, and if I wasn't backed by my superior, I would request relief from that job, which is about exactly what would happen. Anyway, we shall see what happens. But it really gripes me, that in the army, troops are afraid to go to sleep at night for fear of being beaten up. So far, it is mainly in one company, and probably no more than ten or twelve real agitators, with the rest following along.

Anyway, if I have to go on patrol duty in the area, to assist in maintaining discipline, I am going to let it be known that I violently object to acting as patrolman, merely because some hoodlums have not been dealt with appropriately!

I received a letter from Thelma, yesterday. I am already behind with my correspondence. In fact, haven't written anyone, except you, and Colonel B.

I started reading a book by Earl Wilson, *The Show Business No One Really Knows,* and it is interesting. Gives you a look at what really goes on with the people in show business. I think you would enjoy it, so pick it up next time you are at the library.

It has really been hot and humid here this week. Like 100+ for several days. Am thankful for the air-conditioning at night, but could be comfortable with just a fan, as it does cool off at night somewhat.

Well, Darling, that's about all the news from here, right now. Hope you are feeling better each day. As for me, I am feeling o.k. The first couple of weeks here, I had a bug, from the water or something, but it's all right now.

Speaking of bugs, reminds me of the two tiny lizards in the hootch. They try to run on the tile floor, and just sit in one spot, with their legs going ninety miles an hour! They are so comical to watch. As long as they don't get into my food, they are okay! Think I'll catch one and paint his tail, to see if they are the same ones or different ones. They are only about an inch long at the present time, but will grow to about two to three inches long.

It's hard to believe that Easter Sunday is just around the corner! Guess I will be wearing my favorite green "outfit" that day, huh? Doesn't seem too long ago that we were going to church *last* Easter. Anyway, the NEXT one we will be together, right? They are having a sunrise service at 6:30, and I hope I can make it.

I must sign off for now. Remember that I love you, and miss you a whole bunch every day, and think of you ALL the time! Until next time, all my love to you, Darling.

Your Oscar

Sunday 2 April 1972

Hi Darling,

Well, here it is Easter Sunday once again. Hope you got to church, and enjoyed the service. I didn't make it for sunrise service (as you probably could have guessed) but did go to the eleven o'clock service. Easter was declared a holiday for the Vietnamese people, but not for the Americans. I don't mind working since there is little else to do, but I do think the army is being a little ridiculous when it becomes so self-important that it cannot stop for a day such as Easter. What you get from the personnel is a half-hearted effort, anyway.

I was glad to get your shopping list, and will get started on it soon. You are right about us not really needing anything else, but I thought we would get a few tokens anyway. Yes, I think the trays will be excellent gifts, and with proper care will last for ages.

Yes, there are a few things that I need, like multivitamins, something for cuticle, and an electric toothbrush. Go out and buy a new one, and send me the old one, okay? It will flake out one of these days, anyway, so it won't be any great loss.

The news from up north is a little rough today. Maybe by the time you get this letter, things will be settled up, one way or the other. I think things must come to a head, in the next few months, if things are going to be settled. As long as they don't start jacking around with the Americans, they might do all right. If the ARVN don't hold too well, I know a lot of people will be disappointed, and that, of course, is part of their objective, to discredit the government and ARVN, even if what appears to be true, isn't.

I showed the clipping you sent about Long Binh to some of the guys, and they got a kick out of it. Most of what they say is true. There are swimming pools, they are building a theater, they do have floor shows (if you would call them that) at some of the clubs. What they did not say is that most people don't have time, or are too tired to go swimming or clubbing, and that the place is just a large, dirty place. And they do have some prostitutes sneaking around at night, even though it is against the regs. Again, it is the commanders who permit this to go on. Some of them put a stop to it, and others don't care.

Pay records still aren't straightened out. This army is getting to be something else! Any time you want something done right, you just about have to do it yourself! No one seems to care about doing a good job, or doing ANY job, for that matter. Guess it's not just the army, either. I think the American people, by and large, are becoming a bunch of lazy people, who want something for nothing, and when they get it, they are unhappy about it. . . .

Thank you and Vivien for the cookies. They came at noon, and I ate about half of them right then! They were great!

Glad to hear you are back singing in the choir. Wish I could be there to listen.

The chaplain I really like is leaving next week. He is a West Point graduate, and I wanted to find out how he ended up a chaplain, but never did. He is the first WP graduate I know of who is a chaplain.

I'm down to two days a week of PT, and one night of running. First place, I don't have the time, and secondly, am too tired. Seems like my whole life is get up, eat, go to work, come home, read a little, eat, sleep, and then repeat. But as long as I'm able to get up and go, I feel thankful.

Say, Margaret! Ma'Su writes just about as badly as I! It took a while to decipher her letter.

You are so right! I must write to Mom tonight. Should have written sooner. Will write Brenda and Charles, too.

I do miss you a whole lot, especially in the evening, when I come home. Don't have that good feeling that I am going to be with you pretty soon.

My new "roomie" and I get along well. He doesn't come in 'til nine or so in the evening. We say "Hello," talk a little, and then he reads awhile, and goes to sleep.

Time to close the library, so must close. Hope you are in A-1 spirits. Remember I love you, and miss you the most!

Your Oscar

Tuesday 11 April 9:00 P.M.

Hi Darling,

Another Sunday in Vietnam, and letter writing time again. I went to early church this morning, and otherwise have not accomplished anything else.

It was nice of Viv to make up the Easter basket for you. I don't know how she has time to do all those extra things, do you?

Darling, I'm in about as safe a place as there is, over here right now. Nothing is going on at present, but then you know the VC are always full of surprises, so you just go about your business, and try not to worry. You just have to put your faith in the Lord, and let it go at that, right? I'm hoping that I can get another job in about a month, as this one is going to fizzle out pretty soon. At any rate, I want to get something more commensurate with my rank, as right now I'm doing things a LTC has no business doing. It's o.k. for awhile, since there are some other people in the same boat, but not for longer than a couple of months, as it is a waste of talent as far as I'm concerned. What gripes me is that the HQ has a bunch of MAJ's and LTC's who don't really know what they are doing in many cases, and I'm sitting out here with a rinky-dink job. At any rate, I told USARV HQ personnel officer about three weeks ago that I expected to be out of a job here, around May 1, so we will see what happens. I'm hoping to get a job that will last for the rest of my tour, so we can plan on R & R and other things without having to change plans because of a transfer.

At this time, all the LTC's living in the group of trailers where I live are walking guard at night around the area. Some fun! . . . Last night while I was on guard, around 4:00 A.M. the sky toward Saigon lighted up, and there was a tremendous ball of fire and explosion. Guess it was an ammo boat, or a gasoline supply point. It was about six miles away, but a very impressive sight.

A lot of our enlisted men are leaving, so by the end of the month we'll be operating with a minimum of personnel. Some of them are getting out of here having served as little as five to seven months. Pretty good deal – right? I wonder if it really was necessary to send them over for such a short tour.

Sounds as if some of the advisors who are up north have been having somewhat of a rough time of it. I think if the SV can hold them off and move them back, the North will have lost their last gamble, and it may be disasterous for them. I think what they really want is to take a couple of large provinces or cities up north, and then talk peace, since they then will have "saved face." One thing seems pretty obvious, and that is if the SV were as dedicated to their cause as the North, it wouldn't last long over here. At any rate, I'm keeping my fingers crossed for the South Viets.

Yes, I am receiving the Indianapolis newspaper, and I really do appreciate it. However, I don't want you to renew it, as I can read it in the library when I have time, and it will save some poor mailman from lugging some extra weight every day. The *Stars and Stripes* is pretty good over here, and we get good coverage, I think.

Hope you have been able to get the TV repaired by now.

Seems like every time you move, something gets damaged or completely ruined.

How is your family? Hope your father and mother are doing all right.

Sweetheart, if I don't tell you sometime how much I miss you, and love you, just remember that I do, o.k.? Sure seems a shame that NEWLYWEDS like us have to be separated so soon. Guess the best thing to do is just hang in there, and hope the time passes quickly. I do get disgusted, sometimes, and wonder what I am doing over here, so far away from you, and then I get a little blue. How about you? I am convinced that the only solution is to keep as busy as possible, so there isn't much time to think about it.

My eyelids are getting the "droops," so I must close, and hit the sack. I think of you always, and I miss your sweet smile and your loving ways. Know I'm really a lucky guy to have found you!

'Til next time all my love to you.

SHAPE UP!

Your Oscar

Sunday 16 April 5:00 P.M.

Hi Darling,

Was glad to get your letter yesterday, and to hear that you and Vivien made the trip to Houston. I had to laugh when I read that Brenda wanted you to stay for a month. Guess you should feel good about that, as most girls probably are glad to see their mothers leave.

How was the weather on the trip? Right now it is hot and humid, here. The troops are on an alert, so they are probably out there grumbling around. I don't feel sorry for them much, since most of them have had it made on their tour here, but I doubt that they realize it. Some of the advisors are having a hard time of it in some places. I really think the North Viets shot the bolt on this one. I don't see how they can possibly succeed in a military victory in the long run, and they have an awful lot to lose. They can get some success for some time, but not for long, as they don't have the heavy logistical capabilities for that sustained operation, at least that is my guess. So far, they haven't hit Long Binh yet, but everyone is expecting it, as this is the only place they haven't. They might shoot in some large rockets, but that will be all.

Margaret, there is no sense worrying about anything. I am being as careful as possible, and I want to come home as badly as you want me to come home. So, if something does happen, it will be unavoidable. Anyway, we just have to trust in the Lord for the best; so don't worry, okay?

So far, there are very few Americans involved in the operations up here. Have been trying to find out something about my next job, but so far, I haven't had any luck.

As for my health, I feel fine. Last week, I had a real bad stomach for several days. I decided that it must have been caused by some bad water I was drinking every day at one place. It was supposed to be potable water, but at any rate, I stopped drinking it for a couple days, and the stomach ache left. I told the guy in charge, so he had all the tanks cleaned out, and it's apparently okay now.

I shipped a couple of ceramic elephants to you today; probably won't receive them for at least a month.

I got all sharped up in my fatigues this morning, and went to church, at 9:30. When I got there, I found out that the service was at 8:30. I was pretty disgusted, especially since they had put out a big flyer during the week with big letters about an inch high, giving the time as 9:30. I'm glad to hear that you have found a church you like. Speaking of church, have the kids had Robbie and Tommy christened yet? They haven't mentioned it in my letters.

Say, I finally found some lobster tails at the PX, last night, so I cooked a couple. They were pretty good, but I didn't have any butter, so I made up a sauce out of mustard, horseradish, vinegar, garlic salt, and a few other odds and ends — sounds sickening, doesn't it? It wasn't too bad, but not nearly as good as drawn butter. Next time I'll have some, even if I have to mooch it from the mess.

Did you have any good adventures in eating, while on the trip? I'm sure you must have had some good Mexican food, right?

I read in the paper that it is still very cold in Indy. I don't really miss the snow, do you? (I KNOW you don't!)

I do like to sit and think of our evenings, and our nice

dinners that we used to have, and I can tell you that I really do miss all of it. It seems so long until we will be together again, but must bear with it, I guess. Tomorrow will be two months since I left. That is one-sixth of the way, so time marches on. I think of you all the time, and wish that I could do something nice for you. If you can think of anything, please let me know.

If you happen to find some film for the MINOLTA, send me a few rolls, color, if possible. Be sure to mark the package "UNEXPOSED FILM, DO NOT X-RAY."

Darling, it's time to close the office and head for home. Hope this finds you in the best of spirits possible, under the circumstances. Remember that I love you the most, and am thinking of you always. Until next time, all my love to you.

Your Oscar

Wednesday 19 April 1972

Hi Sweetheart,

Was glad to get your last letter, and presume that you had a pleasant and safe trip home. I must say that Robbie sure looks different in the snapshots. From what you say, he is developing into a nice mannered little fellow. I also think that he is going to be a real intelligent boy, from what little I have seen of him. Sounds like Brenda has been spending a lot of time with him.

I know what you mean by being bored with traveling around. No matter how small a home you may have, it is always nice to return to, when you are tired.

I just returned from "supper" at the mess hall, and stayed for a movie. It was a real thriller, *Shoot-out at O.K. Corral* or something like that, but it helped to pass the evening. I have guard duty from 3:00 A.M. to 5:00 A.M., so must try to hit the sack by ten o'clock.

Nothing is going on around here at present. Was glad to see my "Old Buddy," the president, come through and start the bombing up north. Should have done that way back in 1965, then we probably wouldn't be here now. But guess there is not much else he can do. There isn't much fighting around here yet, and don't expect too much, though I guess the heavy fighting in some places will continue for at least three or four weeks more. I hope that by then we can get them moving out, but then, the bad weather will be here. I'm not worrying about it, at any rate, and I hope you aren't.

I received a letter today from COL B. He is planning to retire in the spring, after four weeks evaluation duty at Grayling, two weeks at Ripley, Minnesota and two weeks with the Indiana Guard. Sounds like a hardship tour, huh?

Have found out that I should request R & R time about three months in advance, so what about August? Sounds like a long time off, but if I have to stay here a year, that will be the halfway mark. Thought we might like to take it in Hawaii, but we can take it anyplace you might like to go. Tell me what you want to do. As long as you are there, I don't care! Two weeks of vacation sounds great, doesn't it?

Here, I never see TV, or listen to a radio, and I don't miss it at all. Read the *Stars and Stripes*, and other papers at the library, and that is all I need or have time for.

Guess that is all the news from here. I am in excellent health, and hope you are the same. I know that I am so lucky to have such a sweet, loving, perfect wife, in every way! When you lie down to sleep at night, just remember who loves you the most, and I'll be thinking of you, as always. Your bedtime is about noontime, here, and I always think of you then.

So, 'til next time, all my love to you. SHAPE UP!

Your Oscar

Sunday 23 April

Hi Darling,

Thought I would write you a note, while at the office today, and things are nice and quiet.

Went to church this morning, and it was pretty good. They had some singers, all colored, who were real good, and they jived things up a little, and made it more lively.

I am moving about Wednesday of this week, so by the time you get this, I will be working at my new job. I am supposed to go to the Delta as an advisor, and it sounds like a good deal. That is more my line of work, and I may have a reasonable chance of making COL. There may be some small action down there, but nothing like they have going up north. It is really a mess, huh? I wish they would get things settled and stop "jacking" around!! Maybe I will get a good night's sleep, for a change. I haven't had a day off, since I left you in MS.

Received a letter from Mom yesterday, and she is fine. Don't know how she does it! My brother, Herb, is having some problems, and has had for some time. All that makes me realize that a person should live it up while he can, as once you start getting older, no telling how your health will hold up. I have been feeling pretty good, everything considered.

Had a letter from Viv, also one from Thelma. Guess when it comes to letter writing I'm No. 10! What I need is a secretary!

No more news from here, and that is a good sign. Remember I love you the most, and miss you the same. Take care and have fun whenever possible.

Your Oscar

Thursday 27 April

Hi Darling,

It was great to hear your voice once again, the other day. I don't know when I will be able to call again. I left Long Binh yesterday, and arrived down here at Can Tho early this morning. Can Tho is about sixty miles south of Saigon.

Saw a few people I knew at the compound in Saigon last night. They were on the way home, and I felt like I would like to be going, too.

The way it looks, I am scheduled to be an advisor to the 44th Vietnamese Rangers (a Regiment, three battalions). Right now, I am waiting to be interviewed by the general.

I understand the Rangers are up north, now, so I presume that I will be heading up that way for a while. The Rangers move around quite a bit, and are usually a pretty good outfit. Guess I'll be spending a good deal of time out in the field. Hope all of this makes the time pass quickly.

Right here at Can Tho Headquarters, things are pretty good. Not as comfortable as Long Binh, but okay. They even have a swimming pool in the compound, but I doubt that I'll ever get to use it, if I am out in the field.

I think my time with the Rangers will count as command time, the same as if I were a Bn Cdr of an American Bn. If that is not so, then I am really spinning my wheels. I do hope this mess clears up pretty soon!

I hope you are well. I'm okay, so please do not concern yourself too much, okay? All will be well if we say our prayers, right? Stay as sweet as you are, and remember I love you.

Your Oscar

Sunday 30 April 1972

Hi Darling,

Well, one more week down the drain! Just got back in from the field, where I spent the last three days traveling over most of the northern part of the Delta. I am being assigned to a Ranger group in the Delta. It sounds like a good job, and it should be interesting and keep us pretty busy. The Rangers are usually assigned to a large territory (Military Region) of which there are four. Region I is up north, II and III are around Saigon, and IV, which is in the Delta.

Since the big fracas up north, this Ranger group has been moved up around Hue, or Quang Tri, so I may be going up to join them in a couple of days. Am scheduled to go to Saigon tomorrow, to draw some gear, to get briefed, and arrange transportation for the trip up north. No telling where they will be by the time I get there. Anyway, as an advisor, I should be near the rear, so that should be no problem, and I will be doing what I have been trained to do, so I am not too concerned about it yet. Also, I asked God to send me where I could do the most good, without getting into trouble, so I am happy about it. I should run into some of my old "Compadres" up there, as I know a couple of COL's who are with the Rangers.

I am going to have them hold my mail here for me until I get up there, and find out what the deal is, so I may not hear from you for some time. If you don't hear from me for awhile, don't worry, as the outgoing mail will be a problem for awhile. If some emergency comes up, your best bet is to contact the Red Cross, and they can locate me.

I think my home base will be here at Can Tho, or maybe over on the Cambodian border. Was there last night, and it is really beautiful country: flat land, with many trees, and some beautiful mountains. I would like to travel there in peace time.

I hope I can keep this job at least six months, as it counts as command time, and it should help us out quite a bit when promotion time comes around!

The last couple of days, I've been eating a lot, to fatten up for the "C" rations and Viet food that is heading our way.

Speaking of food, this morning while waiting for a chopper, I saw a VN guard very busy roasting a big fat rat for his breakfast!! I don't know if he cleaned him later or not, but he was roasting him whole! I had not eaten breakfast, and I was glad. The guard had a couple of traps set out in the weeds, so he had to demonstrate for me how he caught them. He seemed pretty proud of himself!

I am sending you a map, showing the places that I mention and our headquarters.

Didn't get to church today, but a chaplain was out in the field yesterday, so we had services then.

I hope you are feeling good, and I do plan to call soon. Remember I love you, and am so sorry that we are apart.

All my love to you, and "Hello" to all the family.

Your Oscar

Thursday 8:00 P.M.

Hi Darling,

Well, I'm still here in Can Tho. Right now, things are a little undecided as to where I will be in the near future, but hope to find out tomorrow. The unit that I was to join, up around Quang Tri, got somewhat disorganized, and the COL who was with them came on back, so I don't know if I will join that particular unit or not. I think they are probably reconsolidating up around Hue, and the next couple of weeks or months will be decisive. At any rate, don't worry about me, as I'll be okay.

I'm going to try to call you tonight, if I can get through.

Hey, I hit the jackpot today on mail call. Received two letters from you, one from Charles, one from Brenda, one from Vivien, and the package. The electric toothbrush is great, and it was good to get to use it. I can use it a lot, if I don't have to spend too much time out in the field.

I really am happy with this job, and know that I am going to like it.

Just in case I forgot to mention it, I requested fourteen days R & R, in Hawaii, starting on 21 August. That is about halfway through the tour, so should be a good time.

I miss you and think of you all the time and wonder

how you are. Do take care of yourself, and start eating better!

Wow, Margaret, the little kids have changed a lot, judging from the snapshots I have received. They are both so cute.

The charm that you sent with your picture is really great! Know where I wear it? On my "Dog Tag" chain! How about that?

Since being here in 'Nam, I have just about come to the conclusion that when I get home, I'll put the TV in storage, as I really haven't missed it at all, except for the news. Just think of all the talks we could have, books to read, other things, instead of TV. But we really didn't watch that much. I will say that it is really great company, when you are alone, as you are now.

The last week has been a "hassle." We were moving almost every day. I will be so glad to put my bags down someplace more permanently.

That's about all the real news from here for now. I send all my love to you, and thank you for being such a wonderful person, and being so nice to me. AND SHAPE UP!!

Your Oscar

9 May 1972

Hi Darling,

Thought I had better write you now, while I have a little time. We are out in the field on an operation, and at present, there is a short lull in the action, so will take advantage of it. I am with the 42nd Ranger Group, and we are presently helping the 7th Viet Division, which is about seventy miles southwest of Saigon. Our home base is just a few miles from the Cambodian border. I spent most of yesterday up in a chopper, air landing troops, watching air strikes, etc. We are to be out here for five days, unless something develops.

We have our Command Post set up in a tin hootch. I've strung up a hammock, and had a good night of sleep, last night. We have been eating "C" rations, which aren't too bad for a few days. I bought a small cooking stove that uses kerosene, for about two dollars, that cooks No. 1! There is a CPT with me, and we just brewed a cup of Constant Comment; courtesy of Miss Margaret!

The mail from now on will not be regular, as all depends on when we get a chopper out here, and someone we can depend on to mail our letters.

I just heard Nixon's speech, and I thought it was outstanding! It's about time we stood up to those Russians, as they have been going "Hog-Wild" for several years.

Wow, Margaret, I am so far behind with letter writing! I need some carbon paper, to put out a bulletin or something.

That little charm with your picture is great! I get to look at you several times during the day and think of you always. Time marches on, and R & R can't come too soon, right?

I hope you are taking good care of yourself, and are able to "goof off" and relax a lot. It must be getting warm there so get out and hit the pool when you can. My tan is just about gone. The weather here is hot and humid, but not too bad at night.

You know how I miss you, and want to be with you, so take care, and SHAPE UP!

'Til next time, all my love to you. Have fun!

Your Oscar

11 April 1972 9:15 P.M.

Hi Darling,

I'm writing tonight, because we are expecting an American helicopter out tomorrow, and hopefully can get our mail out. I think we will be out in the field for at least another week on this operation. We are working over an area, where the government troops haven't been for some time, so we do have plenty of work to do. We are in good shape. Tonight, the CPT fixed up some Spam, from "C" rations, some chopped onions, and we mixed that with some instant rice, and believe it or not, it was pretty good. The Viets are issued instant rice in plastic bags (from the U.S., I think), and all they do is pour in some hot water and let it set for about ten minutes, and they have a rice dinner! Makes the "C" rations taste better, and also last longer.

The weather today is hot and muggy, and it is the dark of the moon.

We are co-located with the Division Command Post, so we are living in a big bunker, which is really o.k. Only bad thing is the big artillery pieces that make a terrific amount of noise, but I'm getting to where I can sleep right through it all. How about that? That's because we are usually so tired that we can sleep anyplace anytime we get a chance.

Let me know if and when you receive some of the things that I ordered through PACEX. I haven't received any confirmation, but my mail is irregular, so can't tell what is really happening.

Are you beginning to look forward to R & R and Hawaii? I sure am, but it seems like a dream at the present time, but it will be here before we know what happened!! (I hope!) It will be great to have nothing special to do, and no schedule to keep, travel the islands and just have fun, right? If Karen and Norman are still there, we might be able to see them and get suggestions about what to see and do.

Now, how are you doing? You never tell me much about how you are feeling. My exercise program has fallen by the wayside at the present time. I have a small fever blister on my lip, and I *hate* them. Maybe some of the pineapple I ate had too much acid.

Not much news from here, except I think of you all the time, and wish to be with you, as you already know.

I pray for you each day, and that you will be okay, and know how much I love just you.

Your Oscar

17 May 1:30 P.M.

Hi Darling,

I just got back in from the field, and was pleasantly surprised to find two letters from you. Needless to say, I read each of them two times, and also enjoyed the letter from Charles, that you enclosed. I am glad that they are enjoying their tour in Europe, and getting to travel a lot.

Thanks for the last snapshots. You are looking great, and I have them pinned up on the wall by a mirror, so now you are my pinup girl! I'm a little disappointed that you are cutting your hair, but I know that it must be uncomfortable when it is so hot. I guess you are one of the fortunate women who look good in either short or long hair.

I am glad to hear that the rings arrived okay. I just hope that they are something like you wanted. I ordered them large on purpose, as I didn't know which finger you would want to wear them on.

You are really getting a variety of work assignments, with Manpower and Kelly Girl, and I think that is terrific. You are getting some very good experiences in a lot of things.

Right now, we are exactly one-fourth of the way through this tour, and we have our R & R to look forward to, very soon.

Right now, I am at our home base, a place called Chi

Lang, which is a few miles from the Cambodian Border. Our Ranger group just finished up a two-week operation south of Saigon about sixty miles, and we drove back yesterday and this morning. We saw some very beautiful country. Also took a ferry ride across the mighty Mekong River on the way. That was a lot of fun, and a relief from the humdrum of the field. We are supposed to be here one more day, and then back out on another operation. They work the Rangers pretty hard, because they are pretty good troops. The ones I am with have been on combat operations for two months now, with only a couple of days off.

We have a number of new people, as they lost some in the Cambodian operation, before I joined them. The last couple of weeks, they made three assault landings with choppers, and had some small victories without getting hurt much, so their confidence is built up pretty good. The Division we were with wasn't too eager to get into heavy contact with the enemy. Actually, they had good contact one day, but they pulled back some, and most of them got away. In a way, I can't blame them. They think, "Well, at least I'll be here tomorrow, and I can fight them then, if I must," or something to that effect. Actually, we have spoiled them pretty much, with all the air and artillery support, not to mention the logistical support.

Everyone in 'Nam, it seems, has something that comes from the States . . . clothes, food, vehicles of some sort, soap, etc., you name it they have it!

The rice, I told you about, comes from Louisiana! Isn't that something? This is the rice center of the world, and we are sending rice over here!

Actually, some of these soldiers are just great. They are technically proficient, eager, cool and brave under fire, but sometimes it happens that some way they lose cohesiveness, and they fall apart. I think it is because of poor leadership at high levels, sometimes, as it happened up at Quang Tri. The CPT working with me was up there, and from what he said it was a mess. I missed it just by two days, and am just as glad, because I would hate to be a party to such a goofed up mess. However, I do not believe that Hue will fall.

You know we have been eating "C" Rations and Viet food for a couple of weeks, and I was looking forward to a good steak or roast beef for lunch today. Guess what? Right, they had chop suey with chow mein noodles!!

On the way back last night, we stopped at an old abandoned airstrip, at Chau Duc, which is about one hour from here. Had my first good night of sleep in about two weeks. We arrived in here around nine this morning, and I spent the entire morning cleaning up my room. Some LTC had left it in a pretty big hurry, and everything was a filthy mess!

The only thing I need over here besides you is a "lumper" to haul my junk around, every time I have to move! Actually the people I work with are beginning to know me, and they do help some, but it does become a nuisance to carry everything we have, every time we move. Here is an example of what we carry: "C" Rations, two radios for communications, some flares and smoke signals, cooking utensils, a bag for clothing, the harness with pack, survival kits, ammunition to include grenades, a pistol, rifle, five-gallon water cans for drinking water, some soft drinks (cokes, etc.) if we have any, and feel like carrying them, a hammock or cot, whichever we prefer, mosquito nets, air mattress, and many other items; but that will give you an idea of how much. I have a mental checklist I go through, but usually forget an item or two. Last time I forgot a mirror, and had to learn to shave without one.

Say, Margaret, I am always thinking of you, and should tell you once in a while how much I love you, admire you, and am extremely proud of you. I just can't imagine myself being married to anyone else in the world but you. I am so proud of you for so many reasons. First, because you are such a wonderful person. You are kind and loving, considerate, efficient, so much fun to be with, and do things with; you are vivacious, interesting, and never boring, always willing to try something new, so thoughtful of others . . . I could go on and on. I truly love you, and am so thankful that we found each other, and am just sorry that we are presently apart. I say a few prayers each day for you, and for the both of us. I truly feel that God is watching over me here, and I am doing my part.

I wish I had the 35mm camera here, as I could get some good color slides. Can't find any film for my little Minolta.

The choppers aren't coming on schedule, so mail might be late.

Thanks for remembering my mom on Mother's Day.

'Til next time, remember you are my whole life, and I love you the most.

Your Oscar

21 May 1972 3:00 P.M.

Hi Darling,

Here it is Sunday once again, and I didn't even know it until the CPT told me! We are back in the field, again, and are operating now on the extreme west-north part of the Delta, on the coast, by the Gulf of Siam. It is truly a beautiful piece of country, by the coast. There are dozens of beautiful, small islands just off the coast, and all very close to each other, in the emerald-colored water. Any place else in the world, they would be highly developed, but there doesn't appear to be anything or anyone on them, at least from the air.

We are inland from the coast, at a place called Chan Lein. The locals here just sat around and watched the enemy take over the village, and burn about half of it down. Now they control most of the town, and a big cement factory.

We came here with the Rangers, yesterday, to try to clean up the area *for* them. I think the troops would rather not fight today, as well as a lot of other days, but they don't have much choice. One thing about the NVA and the VC, they are dedicated and also brave in most cases. Usually, if penned in, you can figure on them giving good resistance!

The "friendlies" vary. In most of the cases, they would

take less casualties if they were more aggressive, and positive, in their operations, and this is one of the problems, I guess.

I'm writing this, sitting on the ground, in the shade of an old tin shed (seems like there is always an old tin shed) where we have temporarily put up our cots and gear. We have moved twice in the last two days, and may move again tomorrow, if we get this cleared up. Right now, there is a lot of fire flying around, but no sweat, all is A-O.K.

Now, that's enough of this *mess* over here; let's talk about you. Hope you are doing fine, and having a nice Sunday. Haven't seen a chaplain around for awhile, so I read the Bible for awhile.

I am glad to hear that you are enjoying the church choir. I wish I could be there to look and listen!

The pictures of the apartment look very nice. Is it large enough for you? Sounds like the resident manager is a very nice lady. Hope you are enjoying the sun and the pool.

You wouldn't believe my hair! Haven't been able to get to a barber in a month, and I've been thinking of tying it up in back! At least, I have something to comb.

Darling, I do so miss you, and you know without my telling you how much I wish to be with you.

There really isn't much to write about from here, except the war, and I'm sure that you hear more than enough of that, so I won't go into detail unless you want me to. As I said before, please don't worry about me, and enjoy yourself.

Haven't had a chance to shop much, but we can do that together, in Hawaii!!

Must get going, so 'til next time, all my love to you.

Your Oscar

24 May 1972 8:00 P.M.

Hi Darling,

I think I had better write you a short note tonight, as we expect a helicopter out tomorrow, to pick up mail.

We are still working on the same operation. Have cleaned up all the trouble around the town, except for a few hangers-on, out in the cement plant here. It is the only "industry" in South Vietnam, so they don't want us to blow it all away. We should have it cleaned up, by tomorrow.

I'm writing this by flashlight, so please excuse the mistakes.

Here, in the evening, since we are near the coast, we get a nice cool breeze.

After this operation, we are to head north, along the coast, on the Gulf of Siam. If we do, we will be able to get some nice fresh shrimp, oysters, and lobster!! I am feeling real good, and enjoying my job. My stomach hasn't bothered me too much, which surprises me. Maybe the "C" Rations are good for it! They aren't too bad, but very *greasy*. We usually mix rice with our meat, have some canned fruit, French bread, and peanut butter or jelly. Actually, the food is nourishing, but I do miss good crisp salads! Yesterday, I had about three-fourths of a quart of fresh cocoanut milk, and cocoanut meat. In the evening, we had some papayas. Also, we can usually get bananas and pineapples. So — it isn't steak and baked potato, but it's o.k.

Tonight I can see just about half of the moon, a few small clouds, real clear skies, and lots of stars.

I hope this letter finds you in great spirits, and feeling good. As you know, I think of you always, and how proud of you I am, and how wonderful you are. . . .

I've been waking up every night around 2:00 A.M., our time, which would be around noon your time. I was wondering if you were trying ESP to communicate with me?

A Vietnamese just walked up, and is standing here, looking over my shoulder. I wonder if he can read English. He hasn't left, so I guess he doesn't. They are great people in many ways, once you get to know them. The ones I am with now treat me real good, and are beginning to be more communicative with me. I hope I can stay here with them a while longer.

Tell all the families hello for me, and I will write whenever I have some time.

I must close, as I have some things to do. Remember who loves you, and is thinking of you, always.

Your Oscar

Saturday 27 May 1:00 P.M.

Hi Sweetheart,

Thought I had better write today, as tomorrow we may be on the move, up the coast for a few miles. At least, there are a few showers there, and an American "John." I flew up a couple of days ago for a briefing, for some helicopters, and during an hour layover, I took a good shower. It was the first shower I've had in a week, and it really felt great!!

Wanta know what I had for lunch? A can of spaghetti, and some grape Kool-Aid! (Ugh.) What a combination!

Today, we are kinda goofing off, getting our equipment and weapons all cleaned up. We think we have this area cleared out of VC; at least things are considerably quieter. People are back in the village, starting to rebuild already.

Today is a nice day: hot with a few clouds, but always a little breeze. I am trying to find a map, so that I can mark it, and you can follow our operations on it. The Delta is all of the area south of Saigon. (Usually considered to start about twenty miles south of Saigon.) It is where the Mekong River goes across the country, and all the south land. Actually, the Mekong has several branches that run generally parallel, and come together and separate at various places.

I think our mail has been misplaced, as I haven't heard from you in almost two weeks, and you said you were writing at least three letters each week.

I plan to write to the R & R Center at Hawaii, as soon as I can find out the address, and ask for the information to be mailed to you. Then you can help me make up our minds about where we want to make reservations. I don't know too much about Hawaii, so we will find out, together, okay?

My PT program has completely ceased, while in the field. We got a good workout, but of a different sort.

Have you heard from any of the group in Indianapolis? I read in the paper about poor Malloy being killed in the trial runs. Guess they are getting just a little too fast for the track. They are running close to two hundred mph.

Right now, I'd settle for something that would go twenty mph! We have to walk almost everyplace, but I guess it's good exercise. Sometimes I get to looking around, and find that I am the oldest person around, even at forty-three! When I finish this tour, I will be willing to spend less time out in the field, unless we are out for fun.

I can tell you again that I miss you. I am happy that you are my wife, and terribly proud of you, and pleased with you. Sometimes I still can't believe it is true. I think you are the most wonderful person in the world. Want you to know that I think of you always, and say a prayer for us, each day.

Tell "all" hello for me, and remember who loves you the most. So, 'til next time, all my love to you.

Your Oscar

1 June 1972 7:45 A.M.

Hi Darling,

We have moved again; now just below the point where Cambodia and S. Vietnam meet on the coast of the Gulf of Siam. It is pretty nice here, but still very far from any other Americans.

We are expecting the pay chopper today, but I don't know if I will get paid or not, with our moving around so much. Actually, I have around one hundred dollars, and at the rate I'm spending it out here, that should last about ten months! I haven't been paid over here yet, except for travel pay, and the dislocation allowance.

We had a seafood feast the first night we arrived here. The CPT and I ate so much, we were sick the next day, and still haven't fully recovered. After eating nothing but "C" Rations for about a month, any other food usually causes problems.

The COL who I was advising was transferred up to the Ranger unit around Hue. He was specifically asked for, by LT GEN Truang, so that is quite a compliment. However, going up there right now while things are pretty hot isn't too good of an idea! They have our people somewhat scattered out, at the present time, so maybe we can stick in for a couple of days, and get some rest.

It's June already, and our tour is one-third over! I'm without you, though, and the time can't pass too quickly. Maybe something will break over here, and we won't have to spend a whole year here. Wouldn't that be great? Just long enough to get in our R & R, get back and get settled down again.

Say, Margaret, if I am not answering some of your questions, it is because I haven't received any mail in two weeks. Actually no one has been getting mail, so guess it's all fouled up someplace. Will probably get a box full, one day soon.

Did you get to see the Indy 500 on TV? I'm glad that Donohue won. You remember that last year he was leading for awhile, until his engine blew out.

What's going on with you, these days? Guess it is warming up considerably, and you will be able to enjoy the pool and get a nice tan. I've lost most of my tan, but hope to get it back before R & R, so I won't have to worry about getting a burn on the beach at Waikiki!

Once again, there isn't much news right now. You know how much I miss you, so just hang in there 'til we can be together again, *for good!*

'Til next time, all my love to you, Darling, and just remember who loves you the most.

Your Oscar

Monday 5 June 1972 6:45 P.M.

Hi Darling,

I'm writing tonight, so that I can get this in the mail, before going back out in the field, tomorrow morning.

It was good to hear your voice last night, but I was somewhat disappointed, because I could not hear you too well. I had to shout, myself, but it was worth it, just to hear you, and know you are okay.

I am mailing a map of this area, to you, so you can get some idea of where we are operating. Hope it can clear up a few things for you. I think I made a mistake on the area I circled as #2, and called it something other than Chi Lang, which is its proper name. I don't think I would ever learn this language, even if I tried, but I guess I should learn a few handy phrases like "Don't Shoot," etc.

As I told you, we got back in for three days, and it was great. The only trouble is that you have to get used to living in the field, all over again. Last month we ate "C" Rations all month, and didn't get any good meat or vegetables, but this time, we are taking canned beans, peas, corn, tomatoes, etc., so we should be in great shape. Had a good steak last night, and will have another in about a half hour, at the airfield club, and then back out about/around 6:30 in the morning.

It is starting to rain almost every day now, and will continue for several months, so must get used to that.

The mail is still fouled up, and I know I am not getting some of your letters.

Hope you are enjoying your assignments, and I know it helps to make the time pass more quickly. When I return, we are going to do a lot of loafing together, okay? Seriously, I'd like to get in some fishing, boating, swimming, etc., wouldn't you? We must *make* time for these things, as time marches on, and we should be doing all of that while we are able.

Did get a lot of reading done the last couple of days, and got caught up on all the news. It's hard to figure out what may happen over here. One of the CPT's told me that the Chinese gamblers are giving 10-1 odds, that the war will be over by July 15, so who knows – maybe they know something. Can't get our hopes high on any such jazz, as it looks as if it isn't going to slow down here in the Delta. They seem to be getting more disorganized, because of new people, inexperience, and young people.

Now, how are you doing? Do miss you a great deal, and wish we were together, as before. I am really looking forward to R & R, which is only about ten weeks away!!! I must confirm the date with my boss, as I will probably become the Senior LTC of the Rangers about August 1, and will have to take over a lot more responsibility.

Say, could you send me some packets of powdered milk, to take with us to the field?

Chow time, so I must go. 'Til next time, all my love to you.

Your Oscar

Thursday 8 June 6:00 P.M.

Hi Darling,

Here I am again! Are you getting tired of my letters, yet? We are back out in the field again, at the place marked on the map, on the Gulf of Siam, at a place called Ha Tien.

It has been pouring rain for a week now, and I do mean *rain*!

This afternoon I made some fruit salad from pineapple, oranges, and bananas. Ate some, and then spilled the rest on the floor by accident, so that was the end of the fruit salad!

I sent the interpreter to the village to buy some cucumbers, sugar, cooking oil, and sweet purple onions. So now, we can have fresh cucumbers and onions. The CPT and I have been sick with some kind of a bug, for about a week, so we went in to see the doctor. He gave us a regular medicine chest in case we get anything else. We have ampicillen, paregoric, combid, kaopectate, etc., so we are now ready for anything!

Today I am writing to the R & R Center, and requesting a packet of information for you, and one to be sent to me. Think it might be a good idea for you to get there a couple of days before me, so that you can become adjusted to the time change, get some rest, and decide if the hotel is o.k.

Thanks for the cookies! I am using the container for a plate. It is just the right size, and since it is clear plastic, I can see any dirt that may be on it, whereas I can't with a mess kit. I did buy some paper plates, but am running short.

I ordered a bunch of things from PACEX, the same time I ordered the rings, but due to the mail foul-up, I have never received confirmation of the order. If and when *anything* comes, be sure to let me know.

I had to buy a new watch at the PX, when I was in. New one has luminous dial, day and date indicator, so I don't need a calendar, and that is great.

I don't know what to get you for your birthday. If it is okay with you, we will get you something real nice while in Hawaii.

Everyone thinks that things may slow down around here for a couple of months. Don't know if it is wishful thinking or not, but think the NVA has been hurt pretty badly, but then who knows? Think Hanoi is going to have second thoughts pretty soon, but right now, they are still "hanging in there."

I miss you, as always, but I think the time may start passing more quickly now. Thank you for being so nice to me always, and loving me.

'Til you hear from me next time, remember who loves you the most.

I love your letters, so keep them coming!! And SHAPE UP.

Your Oscar

Monday 12 June 1972 8:30 A.M.

Hi Darling,

I'm going to write early this morning, before it gets so hot and humid later in the day. I imagine the weather there is much the same as it is here.

For breakfast, this morning, I had some vienna sausage, a couple of fried eggs, and some tomato juice, so I'm in great shape.

We went in to Chi Lang, where we were supposed to have a meeting, but the weather got so bad, the choppers couldn't pick up the other advisors, so it was postponed. We came back out to Ha Tien, early Sunday morning. Everything is quiet, right now. We have lost contact with most of the NVA units we were fighting. Don't know whether they have withdrawn or not. I think that very soon they will revert back to shelling some of the district towns, and taking over some of the smaller outposts, as a form of harassment. Now that things are relatively quiet, we do have some time to read and write letters.

We got a new Vietnamese COL commander, that I advise, and he seems like he is going to be very good. He and a couple members of his staff speak very good English so that makes our communication easier.

On Friday, we took a jeep ride up to the Cambodian

border, where some of the troops were operating. It is truly some beautiful country up that way. So picturesque and peaceful looking.

I would really enjoy taking a trip all over this part of the world, if and when it ever settles down.

On the way, we came to a huge, granite rock, about four hundred feet high, on the edge of a mountain. We stopped and went inside. Most of the inside of it was hollowed out (also the boulder was split) and there were many large rooms, stairs, and a Buddha in a large room. I suppose people have been using this as a shelter for thousands of years. It was really quite fascinating.

The kids come around our "shack" every day to stand around and watch us cook, read, or whatever else we may do. Last night, I played the harmonica for them, and they thought that was really something! It was one of the few times that they shut up! Most of them are still afraid of Americans, as they haven't seen many out here.

I want to tell you about a little character we saw a couple of weeks ago. It happened just after our unit finished cleaning out a village, and the cement plant, where we had some pretty good combat. We were waiting by a small airstrip to be picked up, and as usual some of the small kids were hanging around. There was one urchin, about six or seven years old, who was really fascinating. He would sing at the top of his voice (had a good voice) and dance at the same time. He really had outstanding rhythm, and did every dance step you could ever think of!! He did the Watusi, Frug, Charleston, and a few Balinese steps thrown in for good measure. He had quite a crowd watching, and he truly was very talented. At least everyone got a much needed laugh out of him. In the States, he would be considered a child prodigy, but over here he is just another dirty, little kid, but in spite of all, he seemed to be having the time of his life. Can't help but think of the kids in the States, with the house and garage, all packed full of toys and things, yet they sit around with long faces and gripe!!

Just proves that all the possessions and trappings are worth nothing, if one doesn't have the right mental attitude.

By the way, I must put in my assignment preference very soon, so let me know if you have any ideas. It doesn't really make much difference to me, as long as we are together — Fort Sam, Fort Benning, Fort Ord. Let me know so that we can make some decisions. I am glad that you are doing so well under the circumstances, and that you don't complain. I tell everyone that I have the best wife in the world, and that is for *sure*!!

How is the battle waging between you and the Ford? Keep your eyes open for whatever you would like to have when I get back, or anytime you want it, for that matter.

Guess I must write to the kids again soon, to check them out and keep them shaped up, right?

By the way, if you have something very important or official to send me, send it by registered mail. As I told you our mail isn't completely dependable at present.

Also, when you have time, send me some Camalox or Maalox. No rush, but I could use a couple of boxes. Am using the box and packing that you sent the cookies in to haul eggs out in the field! Time to move, so I must close. Stay as lovely as you are, and I love you.

Your Oscar

Thursday 15 June 1972 3:00 P.M.

Hi Darling,

Thought I would drop you a few lines, even though there isn't much news. The chopper is supposed to show up out here this P.M. to drop us some drinking water. We are still at Ha Tien, by the Gulf. Today the weather is nice, hot, but clear, with a gentle breeze. I am skipping my siesta today, since I stayed awake last night from 1:30 A.M. until five. We usually get to bed around ten or eleven o'clock, and are up about 6:30 or so, depending on what is going on. In the evening there is really nothing to do. Today, I am going to get an electric light rigged up, so we can read at night, if we are so inclined.

Guess what? Just discovered that today, 15 June, is my twentieth anniversary in the army, not counting my two years in the navy!

Listening to the news out here on the radio is one of the highlights of the day. We seldom get the *Stars and Stripes* unless someone gets into HQ. If I ever get command of this outfit, I'm going to make a few changes, if possible. Sometimes I think that some of the Americans just do not realize that we really are going to get out of here, and therefore do not plan accordingly, and that is to phase back in a logical manner.

Have you heard from the kids, lately? Guess they are all very busy, with vacation time and all.

I'm counting the days until R & R! Do you think two weeks is too long for us to spend in Hawaii? If you do, let me know. We can spend a few days visiting some of the other islands, and there are so many things to see and do! By the time you receive this letter, it will only be eight weeks 'til then! We are one-third of the way through now, and if the rest of the time goes as well, I will be satisfied.

From the sound of the news, there may be something brewing with Hanoi, but I don't even like to think about it anymore, as we usually get disappointed, right?

Hope you are all right, and slowing down a little. We *all* must learn to slow down and take time to enjoy life — what little we can. I don't think the Good Lord intended for people to spend their whole lifetime on earth, just running around spinning their wheels, do you? Anyway, I'm getting better at goofing off all the time, and you better get started, if you want to keep up with me! Really, I am learning to relax more, at least until the shooting starts.

Well, Miss Margaret, I must close, and try to get some things moving here. Remember who loves you the most, and wants to be with you, too!

Your Oscar

Monday 19 June 1972 9:00 A.M.

Hi Darling,

Here it is Monday morning again, though you would never know it, as all days are the same.

Last night, the new COL gave a party, and invited most of the local dignitaries. It was a pretty good party, at least different. We had fish fondue, salad, chicken soup, and two roasted pigs, that were beautiful and tasty. They were golden brown, and whoever baked them really knew what he was doing. Anyway, I ate enough to last a few days, as we rarely get any fresh meat, unless we go in to HQ. On the market, we buy onions, cucumbers, bananas, pineapple, and eggs, plus some assorted fruits, if we want them.

We were going up the river about twenty miles today, to check out a unit, but I decided against it as right now the river isn't too secure, and there is no sense in toying with trouble.

I'm enclosing a clipping from the *Stars and Stripes*. The author makes some things sound worse than they are. The part circled is the operation I told you that we were on. Right now our troops have lost contact, and have not regained it, so things are kind of slow here, though I'm not complaining!! We have quite a supply of reading material, so we are in great shape. Yesterday, I rigged up an electric light, so we are getting to be somewhat sophisticated! Also, we have a shower, and can bathe daily. We send our clothes into a little village laundry, and they do a real good job, starch, press, and all; costs about twenty-five cents per uniform, and that is not bad, since we do not furnish anything.

I do hope that the time is passing reasonably fast for you. The days seem to drag, but the weeks are moving by, and we will soon reach the halfway mark. I should find out by July 15 when our R & R will be for sure, as that is when the R & R roster comes out for August. If I ever get into Can Tho I will call you again, providing they still have the phone service. If you need any money let me know, as I can stop the Soldiers Deposit. I don't want you to be skimping on anything.

Wish I had a boat here, as the Gulf of Thailand (Siam) is so inviting looking! I checked the water the other day, and it was real warm. Maybe it is because the water is shallow for a long way. You can walk out about a half mile some places, though I haven't tried it. A little speed boat would be great here, but a mini-bike would be more sensible and handy to get around in, and run errands, cheap to operate, and small enough to take with you wherever you go. I would like to have one over here!

Too bad Gertie and Chester won't be in Hawaii when we are. I admire them for going as they do.

I do miss you a lot, and hope we can make up for all the lost time, when I can come back to the U.S. I am proud of you, and I love you the most.

So – until next time take care. All my love to you.

Your Oscar

Wednesday 21 June 1972 3:00 P.M.

Hi Darling,

At last we got mail!! Yesterday, I received three letters from you, and they all brightened my day, considerably. Enjoyed the other letters from family and friends, that you enclosed. Say, Margaret, why are you saving my letters? I thought you never did that.

I want to try to answer some of your questions. No, advisors are not volunteers, as the article stated. We have been assigned just as any other job, though one just might be able to get out of it, if one tried hard enough. Yes, we were in combat for about a month, when I first arrived here, but things are pretty quiet around here right now, and it looks like it may stay relatively so for awhile, but never can tell.

No, we do not do much walking now. We usually go by helicopter, and set up a base of operations, and work from there. As advisors, we try to encourage the Viets to do what *we think* they should do, but of course we aren't always right, either. Also, we can help them to get some U.S. assets, such as air strikes. When we are not in combat there isn't much to do. I am expecting to be pulled back to HQ, in a few weeks, to Chi Lang, where our higher HQ is. Right now, the CPT and I are the only Americans within fifteen or twenty miles. Our advisors (Ranger Advisors) team only calls for 3 LTC's, 1 CPT, and a SGT. So we will probably have to pull back out of the woods, and consolidate our people somewhat. That will be okay with me, as a few months out here is enough for awhile.

The CPT with me is single, twenty-five years old, with about two and a half years in the army, and he is a good trooper. His folks live in San Diego, but they have lived all over the world, as his father was formerly employed by Standard Oil Co.

Sorry to hear that the jewelry chest was broken. Don't worry, we will buy you a better one in Hawaii, or the U.S.

Did you receive the large, oval brass table, yet?

Thanks for sending the snapshots, but I am returning them, as I might lose them, or get them soiled. Seeing them reminded me how cold it was! It is hard to imagine it, as it is so hot and humid here. It also reminds me of the bottles of champagne that froze and bursted!!

You mentioned about having a tension problem, and asked me if I ever felt like that, and the answer is *Yes*, many times. I'm sure it happens to most everyone sometimes, and I know what you mean about fighting it constantly. It seems to me that fighting it simply intensifies it. When I get that feeling, I try to get very busy, and think of anything else but that. Actually, I think there is a reason for this type feeling, but I don't know what it is. Really, I think rushing and pushing oneself is the main reason. I believe a person must force himself to slow down and live the day for that particular time, and worry about the next day, when it gets here, and take no thought about past problems. Usually, when I am tense, it is because I am anticipating something, or trying to beat some deadline. Actually, I sincerely believe in one way or another, we "borrow" trouble, and should do like the Bible says, and take no thought for tomorrow, as sufficient are the problems of the present day, or something like that. Anyway, Sweetheart, you are no different from anyone else, as this is a pretty common malady of the modern times. Just hang in there, and pretty soon, we will be together, and it always helps to know the other person understands, and sympathizes, which I do, 'cause I have had those same feelings. Just keep in mind that after a while, it will pass. But it is literally a pain in the neck!

The last two weeks, I have been eating just about all the time! Had lost some weight, but think I am just about back up there, now. Guess I had better lay off the bananas!

Guess I'd better stop for now, and get some work going. Take care of yourself, and start learning how to goof off, as the retirement years are getting close, and we can start to relax more, and do whatever we want to!! How about that?

Remember who loves you the most, and wants to be with you. 'Til next time, all my love to you.

And SHAPE UP!!

Your Oscar

Monday 27 June 1972

Hi Darling,

Today, I received a couple of your letters from May! Guess I gave you the wrong Advisory Team address, which is 96, instead of 69!!

Sorry about the trouble with the ceramic elephants. Glad only one was damaged, though. The P.O. would not insure them. Oh, I received the package with all the goodies in it. They will all come in handy, and should last for awhile. Thanks a lot, as I know it is a lot of trouble to go and gather it all up, wrap it and mail it, so I do want you to know that I appreciate it.

Received a happy "Grandfather's" day card from Grandson No. 2. Wasn't that nice?

I haven't received my brochure from the R & R Center, yet. Will let you know the details, as soon as I find out.

We came in to Chi Lang for two days, and are going back out to a new place tomorrow. Things have been too quiet lately, to suit me, but am not complaining – just wondering!

The COL in charge is leaving in about five weeks, and unless another senior officer comes in, I will most likely take his job. That would be fine with me, because then

I wouldn't have to spend so much time *way out* in the boonies.

We are losing two LTC's, and we are only authorized three, so unless someone comes in soon, I will be by myself.

Guess the president will make a speech soon and *should* be cutting out some more people from here.

Sometimes it is so easy to get discouraged over here. Seems like a never-ending turmoil, but I am hopeful that maybe one more big battle will get us out of here.

You asked how much I weigh now. Don't really know, but my trousers are all too big, and I think I look thinner. When you get the "bug" over here that's good for a four to five pound loss, right there. One of these days, I will have had them all, and should be in good shape.

Today is what we call a "BLAH" day here. One of the officers has a sign up in his room that reads "POW'S NEVER HAVE A GOOD DAY." We know that, for sure.

Tell Viv that I received her letter, and will write soon. Also got a letter from Mom. She and a couple of friends are going to a cabin on the beach for vacation. Sounds like she is doing all right. She sent "Thanks" for the money you sent for Mother's Day.

I am o.k. here, and pray that you are the same. Just remember this: *7 weekends until R & R time!!* Do miss you so much, and am so sorry we are apart. But time will pass. Remember who loves you the most.

'Til next time, all my love to you.

Your Oscar

P.S. The popcorn was great!!

30 June 1972

Hi Darling,

I'm writing to you today, just in case the plane comes out. As I told you in the last letter, we are back out in the field in a new place, this time. We are cleaning out an area, where the VC have been for a couple of months. We should have the job done in another couple of days.

Spent most of yesterday flying. I got real cold up there, and had to sit by a fire and drink a hot cup of coffee when we got down. Can you imagine sitting by a fire in VN?

I am advising a different Ranger unit now, and they treat us real good. They feed us, so I'm not doing much cooking anymore; just open up cheese and crackers for breakfast.

You asked in one of your letters about a "lumper." A "lumper" is somewhat like a Redcap, someone who lifts up junk and carries things and moves things for you. It is a term they use in trucking companies.

I just heard the president's news conference, and was waiting for the big word. At least, if they start the peace conference in Paris on the thirteenth, they must have a little something going, huh? Guess they will cut out 5,000 this month, and 5,000 next month. Really, most of them will come from larger U.S. HQ, I think. I don't think it will affect us too much down here.

Hope you are feeling better these days. As for myself, am in great shape, and feel fine. Today, if I can find time, I must write Charles and family a short letter. Sounds as if he is pretty busy, but I think he enjoys this job, don't you?

In case you didn't get my last letter, I think we will start our R & R at Fort DeRussy, and go from there to something else, if we don't like it. When I find out exactly when it is, and when I'll be there, I'll let you know, and you can make reservations better than I, because of the "fouled up" mail situation here. I will send you some extra copies of my orders, when I get them, which will probably be the last part of July. June went by reasonably fast, and I hope July will pass as quickly!

I never did order Thelma anything from PACEX, but I will the next time I go back in.

I hope by the time you receive this, I will have talked with you via MARS, to wish you a "Happy Birthday." Next year we will celebrate both ours together, O.K.? (And then forget them!) I think we should both stay about the same age, from here on in, right?

Sweetheart, you know how much I miss you, especially our nice evenings, and weekends. I was thinking that we two have really had some fun times in the short time we have been married, and a *LOT MORE TO GO*!!

I must close for now, but remember someone way over here in Vietnam loves you the most, and I think you are the best woman in the whole world!!

Until next time, all my love to you.

Your Oscar

Sunday 2 July 1972

Hi Darling,

This will be a short note, since I just wrote a couple of days ago, and there isn't much news.

We are still at Phuc Xuyen, a little place on the map, about forty miles north of Can Tho. There is nothing out here except a small hamlet, and a lot of VC, up the canal, but they are behaving pretty good. Think we will be here a few more days.

You asked about bringing clothes for me for R & R. You can bring several knit slacks, some shirts, and something to dress up in. Have heard that almost every place is very informal. Whatever else we need, we will buy, O.K.?

Time is getting short for R & R, and it gives us something to look forward to. It should be a great vacation.

Are you still riding the bike every day? Those bikes are almost worn out, so we will get us each a good one when we get settled again.

Thank you again for the fine articles in the "CARE" package. The foot spray is really great! ALL the things you sent were real good choices, and I know a lot of them were hard to find, so thank you very much, and for being so nice to me.

Well, Dear, not much news, as you know – still the

same frustrations, dirty war, unenthused people, but I'm sure it will all be over in about two more months, so we must hang in there.

Remember who loves you and thinks of you all the time.

Your Oscar

5 July 1972

Hi Darling,

Hope this letter finds you A-O.K., and enjoying each day as much as you can.

We are still at Phuc Xuyen. Thought we would be gone from here, but the VC are stubborn, and our people aren't too eager, so it is taking longer than it should. At midnight, on the third, the VC fired a few rockets in here to help us celebrate the fourth of July. Then, in the evening, the VN officers dug out a jug of "Snake Whiskey," (which is really a rice wine) and we all had a little drink to celebrate the fourth. Then before going to bed, we fired off some flares, just like the "Arkies" back home, huh?

Every afternoon and some evenings, we have some rain, and it gets comparatively cold. Most days we usually have some sun, which makes it o.k. Today, I got ambitious and did some laundry! Showers aren't too frequent, though there is one that we use down by the canal. When we move around often, depending on where we are, it can be nice, or raunchy. Most of the time, it is "raunchy"! By the time R & R rolls around, I should have most of my bad field work behind me!

I wrote to Charles and Brenda and families, and Mom,

so I'm doing pretty good in the correspondence department.

So far, we haven't been paid this month. Guess the finance officer figured it was too far to come out! Anyway, it gives us something to complain about, which makes us feel better!

In about ten days, the booking roster should be out, for August R & R's, so will send you the poop as soon as possible.

I really can't believe that the summer is about half over. I'm really looking forward to getting home just before Christmas, this year! Wouldn't that be great, to just finish out ten months, and get home around December 15? Guess that is just wishful thinking.

Not much news, so guess I will say "Sayonara." I know I must repeat a lot of things, and you must get tired of reading the same old junk.

Just remember who loves you the most, and thinks of you *all of the time*!!

'Til next time, all my love to you.

Your Oscar

Monday 10 July 1972

Hi Darling,

Hope this finds you in good spirits, and feeling o.k. As for me, I'm in great shape. I intended to write Sunday (yesterday), but was very busy all day. We had a B-52 strike yesterday morning. I'll explain the procedure that we employ when this happens. Right after the strike, we go in with helicopters, to see what the damage is. If we get shot at then, if we have any tactical air available, we call them in, and bomb some more, which is what we had to do yesterday. Then, if things are reasonably quiet, we get helicopters, and airlift in a Bn. of three to five hundred men, to go in and search over the area, and see what they can find. Most all of this time, I am up flying around in a helicopter, controlling the operation. So — that's how I spent *Sunday,* instead of going to *church*! Anyway, all has gone well so far. Guess we can expect more of this type operation in the future. I *still* think this MESS will quiet down, and be over by the end of August. Speaking of August — should find out any day now, about R & R. Thought I would get in to call you for your birthday, but no luck! I want to tell you that I really enjoyed your last long letter, and it lifted my morale considerably! You write nice, "newsy" letters. Reminds me that I must write to Combs!

As soon as I can, I'll make out our preference statement, and put Fort Sam No. 1, Fort Benning No. 2, and Fort Ord No. 3, which is near Monterey, California. We may end up in Washington, which I don't think I would like, as for the work, but the tour might be fun, otherwise. Actually, any place will be okay, as long as we are together, and in good health, right?

Hope you had a nice trip to Biloxi. I always liked the white sand on the beach there, and the beautiful old mansions back off the highway. Guess that is the "old" Mississippi.

The CPT with me has an Instamatic Camera, and has been taking some pictures. If he gets them all developed here, maybe I can send you some copies. We don't look very handsome these days, didn't have a shower for ten days, and lost my deodorant so no one really crowded me for room!! But, here, have had a bath (two gallons of water), found my deodorant, so now I am back among the more civilized way of living. We have been out at this *dinky* little place for two weeks, and we are ready for a move.

Guess I'll round up the barber today, and get a trim job, as the hair is beginning to tickle my neck. Don't have much on the top of my head, but the back is terrific!

Think I'm going ding-a-ling out here??

I want to tell you that it is really nice of you to include the letters you receive from various people, so that I can keep up with all the latest news. I should write a few letters, and will, if and when I get in to where there is a typewriter. How's that for a good excuse?

When I leave here, I will be a MASTER at dreaming up excuses for not doing things, and being evasive, as I am studying with the *masters of all times,* I think. When the VN don't want to do something, or *want* to do something, they can come up with more reasons than you could ever dream of!! At any rate, it accomplishes the purpose for them.

It's time for the Democratic Convention, this week. I think the North Viets may be ready to negotiate, if it looks like the president is a "shoo-in."

Once again, not much news except the fighting, which is going pretty regularly down here, and that is not news. I'm getting to be a peace-loving man, more and more, each day.

Of course, you know I love you a great deal, and miss your company more than I can say. Am really looking forward to Hawaii and MISS MARGARET! Won't believe it 'til we are there, right? We have a saying here – *"Don't be too sure of where you are going until you are there."*

Anyway, I want you to know that I think you are the greatest, most gracious and lovely lady in the whole world, and I am awful proud that you are my wife. Not only do I love you, I like you, too! Now there is a difference!

I must close out, and get to moving. Until next time you hear from me, all my love to my Sweet Baby.

Your Oscar

14 July 1972

Hi Darling,

Received your letter of 7 July, today. We came in to Can Tho, for a couple of days, and got our mail, early.

Feels so good to get a shower, and a *steak*! We have been eating with the VN officers in the field, and have had rice and fish every day. Actually, I like the way they prepare the fish. Good thing, too, or I would be going hungry!

I tried to call you last night, and will try again, tonight and in the morning. After getting your letter, I figured you were in Texas or Louisiana.

Good news! Our R & R is approved to begin on 21 August, for fourteen days! I will arrive on the twenty-first, I think, but will verify that later. Should have the copies of the orders to you in about two weeks from now. I'm hoping to start on a suntan next week, when we go out in the field, but will probably be too busy, and have too much rain.

We cleaned up the "thing" at Phuc Xuyen, so we will be going to Cai Cai next week. That is up in the NW corner, near the Cambodian border.

Sounds like Charles and Mayvene will get home from Germany shortly after I do, providing I leave a little early. Wouldn't it be nice if we were all off at the same time?

Darling, I'm glad that you are enjoying your jobs with Manpower, and Kelly Girl. You are getting a lot of good experience, and they are all interesting and challenging. Most important, it helps to make the time pass quickly.

Still not too much news from here. I'm in good shape, and enjoying the sunflower seeds. Was eating some in the helicopter, on the way in yesterday, and throwing the hulls out the chopper door.

You know who I love more than anyone else does, so take care, and SHAPE UP! Speaking of shaping up, I weighed in at 153 yesterday. I had my weight down pretty good, but two weeks of rice and fish heads, and I'm back up there. So, I better be the one to shape up, huh?

Too bad you and Vivien got sunburned on the beach. Sometimes you can never tell about the sun.

I must close, and head for the club to eat.

'Til next time, all my love to you.

Your Oscar

P.S. Hope I can get you on the telephone tonight!!

18 July 1972

Hi darling,

We are expecting a chopper in about a half hour, so I want to get this letter on it.

I guess you went on the trip last weekend, as I tried to call several times, but no answer. The MARS set-up is pretty good in Can Tho, so I will try again in a couple of weeks, when I get in again.

In case you didn't receive my last letter, our R & R is approved for fourteen days, starting 21 August! I should get the orders off to you next week.

Sweetheart, do you remember when I told you that I was up for promotion in the Regular Army to LTC, and if I didn't make it, we would have to get out in one and a half years? Well, the Good Lord is watching over us, as I made the list, so we can take our time getting out, as I can stay in seven and a half more years, if we like!! How about that? Even if we decide to get out soon, it is nice to know that we could stay on if we wanted to. About one out of four RA LTC's didn't make it, so I feel fortunate. Competition gets stiffer, each notch up the ladder, huh? Anyway, congratulations to us!!

Right now we are at Cai Cai, a little jerkwater joint up by the Cambodian border, north and west of Can Tho, about eighty miles. I think we may stay here about a month or so.

At lunchtime, I'm going to start working on my tan. I stayed out only twenty minutes yesterday, and got a little sore, so I will slow it down a bit.

Enough about me, now how are you doing these days? Can't believe that R & R is so *close*. Then we will have coming home to look forward to, and being together, *always*, right? I think of you constantly, and wish we were together.

Say, Margaret, are Brenda, Robert and Robbie okay? Haven't heard from them lately, and just wondered. Wrote Viv a letter this morning, so I'm all caught up, for once!

I know you must be writing a lot! I do appreciate the nice long, interesting letters you write to me, and I love you for it. It will be nice when we can all be close enough to call on the telephone, or visit over a weekend. You know I am proud to be married to you, and I feel like we have a real wonderful family, with the kids, and I'm part of it. I really like the feeling, so I'm afraid you are stuck with me!

Don't worry about me, as I'm in good shape, and taking good care of my fat little body. Ha!

Until you hear from me again, just remember who loves you the "mostest" in the *whole* world.

Your Oscar

I LOVE YOU FOREVER!!!

25 July 1972

Hi Darling,

I'm a bit late in writing, as I was waiting for copies of our orders to send to you. Thought I would get to mail this today or tomorrow, but no chopper is scheduled, so it will be later than anticipated. Will send you a couple copies in another letter to be sure you get them. You might Xerox a couple copies, just in case you need extras. Time is rolling on! Can't believe that we are getting so close. From what I understand, I will arrive early in the morning of 21 August, but I will probably call you before, so we can coordinate our plans.

We came in for a couple of days, to move all our things again, as we are moving all our personal junk back to Can Tho. I am supposed to be back out in the field in a couple days, for some more operations. So — most of the time in this trip was spent in moving. I hope to get in around payday, if possible.

Thanks so much for the package with the film and stuff.

How was your trip to Texas? Hope you didn't get too tired, and are rested up by now.

Say, how do you like this green pen? Got to digging around, and found this green one, and three red ones, so from now on my letters will look like Christmas!!

Things have been relatively quiet down here for awhile. Makes me wonder what is going on. Hope they don't have any big surprises that would mess up our R & R, right? Guess I shouldn't be complaining when it is quiet, right?

Was glad to receive your letter from Texas. Hope the kids are in good shape, all well and happy.

Well, Margaret, I do miss you, as always, and sure am looking forward to seeing you soon! I don't know how I will act, around a real LADY, again! Anyway, we are going to have two weeks of wonderful fun, right? I am really starting to get anxious now, aren't you?

Guess that's the news from here. I need to take a shower, and hit the pad.

Hope this finds you A-O.K., and in the best spirits.

Remember who loves you the most, O.K.?

'Til next time, all my love to you, my sweet Baby.

Your Oscar

July 29, 1972:	Notified Missing in Action
August 3, 1972:	Notified Killed in Action when helicopter was struck by heavy artillery on July 29. SVN troops reached wreckage and recovered remains on August 2.
August 7, 1972:	Remains arrived in Oakland, California.
August 9, 1972:	Remains arrived in San Antonio, Texas.
August 10, 1972:	Military Funeral at Fort Sam Houston, Texas.

To Margaret –

Upon a warm and summer day, my thoughts are all of you,
And how it feels to be away, from the one I love so true.

A lingering smile, a quiet yes, all echos of days gone by,
And remembered times of happiness, bring forth a mournful sigh.

Our hearts were close, our minds as one, as wintry days slipped past,
Together wondering thither and yon, determined that all would last.

But a time must come, it always seems, for delightful things to end,
To fit as part of the MASTER'S scheme, our lives to better blend.

The time to part, a moment of dread, was greeted with heavy heart,
Wasn't long before I began to feel completely forlorn, and all alone.

Then slowly, I began to comprehend, that a love as strong as this,
Could never really end, but only grow stronger, with nothing amiss.

Though we are so far apart, you are oh, so close to me,
I'll carry you always in my heart, so with me you will always be.

Though I miss your kind and loving ways, more than I could ever say,
I'm counting the months, the weeks, the days, to that time not far away.

When we will come together again, to part — no, nevermore,
And we can then once more begin, our lives, as one, as before.

I'll hold your hand, and kiss your tears, and cry some little, I'm sure,
But then, our doubts, our dreads, our fears, all need no more endure.

And you will know that I need your love, much more than ever before,
And I'll always thank the Lord above, for loving you more . . .

Written in Vietnam, in 1972, by LTC Oscar Herrgesell, who was killed in action on July 29, 1972. The unfinished poem was found in his briefcase, when it was delivered to Mrs. Herrgesell. He was buried at Fort Sam Houston National Military Cemetery, on August 10, 1972.